The Ladder

 ension

The teacher was dressed in his Sunday best and when the student asked him why, the teacher responded, "To celebrate the great feast!"

"Aren't you confused, Teacher?" asked the student. "We just celebrated Ascension Thursday yesterday."

"Yes, that was indeed a high holy day of the Risen Jesus ascending into heaven," replied the teacher. "But forty-one days after Easter is the equally holy, incarnational feast of Descension Friday. After ascending to his reward in heaven, Christ immediately descended deeply into the depths of daily life here on earth. And Descension Friday, I assure you, is a far harder feast to live out than Ascension Thursday."

"Even those who would rather "dance in Sarah's circle" than "climb Jacob's ladder" will agree that a ladder is useful for going down as well as up.... Hays leans his ladder firmly on Jesus, who is not only the ground and the summit of this climb, but the one whom we meet on every rung. Readers who are willing to step on this amazing ladder will find that it is no escalator ride but an engaging, humorous, and most importantly, challenging journey into the heart of life."

— **Robert Hamma,** author *Landscapes of the Soul*

"This newest volume from the pen and creative heart of Fr. Ed Hays is filled with the author's creative, unitive wisdom. Through the medium of ascending and descending a ladder, Father Ed offers us tongue-in-cheek wisdom from the sayings of desert ammas and abbas out of his own creative in-depth musings. Amma Ananda offers pearls to be carried in the heart . . . gems like the golden nuggets one uncovers in reading the sermons of Meister Eckhart. "The Goat's Hair Monk" is a favorite — a must-read!

Like Jesus, our Way, Fr. Ed has tried in this volume to turn our minds upside down while our expectations and past learnings fall short and pale in the glow of Truth and Wisdom."

— **Pascaline Coff, O.S.B.,** foundress Osage Monastery, former Secretary of M.I.D. (Monastic Interreligious Dialogue)

"This astonishing collection of parable stories by the inimitable poet-priest Edward Hays is brimming over with insights into the nature of faith, grace, sanctification, and personal transformation. Throughout his career, Hays has consistently been a pioneer, manifesting a daring mystic sensibility and an unbridled imagination that makes everything seem fresh and new. This is his best book yet. Savoring its manifold riches is bound to make readers feel like they have just struck a deep vein of spiritual gold!"

— **Frederic and Mary Ann Brussat,**
     authors *Spiritual Literacy* and *Spiritual Rχ*

The Ladder
by Edward Hays

Parable-Stories of Ascension and Descension

FOREST OF PEACE
Publishing
Suppliers for the Spiritual Pilgrim
Leavenworth, KS

Other Books by the Author:
(available from the publisher)

Prayers and Rituals

Psalms for Zero Gravity
Prayers for a Planetary Pilgrim
Prayers for the Domestic Church
Prayers for the Servants of God

Parables and Stories

The Gospel of Gabriel
The Quest for the Flaming Pearl
St. George and the Dragon
The Magic Lantern
The Ethiopian Tattoo Shop
Twelve and One-Half Keys
Sundancer
The Christmas Eve Storyteller

Contemporary Spirituality

The Old Hermit's Almanac
A Lenten Hobo Honeymoon
The Lenten Labyrinth
Holy Fools & Mad Hatters
Pray All Ways
A Pilgrim's Almanac
Secular Sanctity
In Pursuit of the Great White Rabbit
The Ascent of the Mountain of God
Feathers on the Wind

The Ladder

copyright © 1999, by Edward M. Hays

Library of Congress Cataloging-in-Publication Data

Hays, Edward M.
      The ladder : parable-stories of Ascension and descension   /
            Edward Hays.
         p. cm.
      Includes index
      ISBN   0-939516-46-2 (pbk.)
      1. Spiritual life—Christianity—Miscellanea.   I. Title.

  BV4501.2 .H36882 1999
  242—dc21
                                                            99-052873

published by
Forest of Peace Publishing, Inc.
PO Box 269
Leavenworth, KS 66048-0269 USA
1-800-659-3227
www.forestofpeace.com

printed by
Hall Commercial Printing
Topeka, KS 66608-0007

pictogram art and cover design by
Edward Hays

Dedication

This book of parable-stories
is dedicated to

Brian Colombe

who for over twenty-five years
has been my friend
and companion climber
on the Ladder
of Life.

"Teacher," asked the student, "why are true friends so rare these days?"

"Because," the teacher answered, "friendship is so expensive"!

Your head is the Ladder;
Bring it down under your feet.

—Jelaluddin Rumi
thirteenth century Muslim mystic

Table of Contents

THAT WHICH IS UNSEEABLE TAKE UP THE

ABLE TO SEE

LINEAR THINKING CAN

ONLY TAKE YOU SO FAR

SO TO GO BEYOND AND TAKE DELIGHT IN BEING PART OF PARABLE THINKING IN HOLY LOOPS...

12

Introduction

"I don't have much time. Just give me the facts." This is a common request of today's hurried people. If someone asks you for directions or for the answer to some problem, he or she does not want you to respond, "Let me tell you a story." Who in search of information today has time to unravel puzzle-tales, cryptic riddles and mystifying stories?

Stories are for children! While that's true, adults also love stories. Indeed, harried adults want *user-friendly* solutions to their problems and questions, but they are also hungry for a good story. No matter how sophisticated or well-educated we may be, we never lose our taste for stories.

A parable is a special kind of story that feeds the hunger of the soul. Yet parables satisfy our hunger in a paradoxical way. They often seem not to make sense. They turn the mind's favorite, familiar, linear paths into labyrinths.

It's precisely by turning inside out or upside down our established thinking patterns that parables provide new solutions to old problems. Parables take the mind on detours from its preferred pathways. Rather than the mind's linear track, parable-stories take us on a loop-the-loop fun ride that forces us to rethink our problems. Instead of a logical process that tries to *break up* a problem into smaller pieces — which are then reassembled into a workable solution — parables lead us toward a *breakthrough* to a new level of understanding.

The mind's usual footpath is paved with the attitude, "If it ain't broken, don't fix it." However, this smoothly paved way may be a dead end or may endlessly lead to nowhere. Moreover, traveling only this well-worn trail prevents us from exploring the uncharted world of What-can-be.

Jesus, along with the Desert Mothers and Fathers, Zen masters, mystical rabbis, Sufi teachers and other great spirit-guides, have always pointed us toward the Promised Land of What-can-be. These teachers often told their students parable-stories to break open the crust of conventional thinking that keeps us in the Woeful World of What-is. The What-is world is a stable, flat world with no horizons, and so to discover the new world of What-can-be requires ascending or descending the ladder of parables.

This book of parable-stories is intended to be just such a ladder for you. Sometimes these tales will take you beneath the surface of your problems, into the heart of the matter where wisdom and clarity reside. At other times, they will raise you above and beyond your difficulties and suffering, to gracefully transcend the gravity of the moment's pain.

Indeed, the hunger for good stories today is just as strong as it was two or three thousand years ago. May these twenty-first century parables, written in the Wisdom tradition of the Desert Father Abba Syah and the Desert Mother Amma Ananda, feed your soul's hunger. May these stories be desert bread, daily manna. At the same time, may they be a Jacob's ladder helping you ascend and descend into the What-can-be world, the kingdom of God beyond and within the world in which we live.

⟩→ CAUTION ←⟨

This Ladder of Parables Is Not an Escalator! Climbing the Ladder Will Require Effort!

The parable-stories you are about to read will present the same challenge as climbing a ladder — personal effort.

Traditionally, good storytellers do not explain their stories lest they spoil the unique application for each listener or reader. In time, the nut cracks open from the inside.

In some of the following stories the author has provided a brief reflection, which may help keep you moving on the parable path. Yet if you find yourself stuck on a particular parable rung, even if it has an author's reflection, remember that a ladder is not an escalator. As the Islamic mystic Rumi said, "Bring your head down under your feet and begin climbing."

⟩→ WARNING ←⟨

While such a position as Rumi suggests is enlightening, it can cause dizziness and even social or religious disorientation.

The Discovery of
Abba Syah's
Sayings of Jesus

The writings of Abba Syah (*pronounced* Sigh-ah) were
discovered in Egypt on December 31, 1999, at exactly
11:59 P.M. At that last minute of the millennium, a
multinational team of archeologists was celebrating
New Year's Eve inside the crumbling ruins of an
ancient Coptic monastery where they were conducting
a study.

The discovery of these previously unknown manuscripts of Abba Syah was the result of a freak accident: While opening a champagne bottle, the flying cork struck the ceiling and dislodged a small section of the fragile ceiling plaster. At the source of the trail of the falling plaster dust, one archeologist saw the protruding edge of a bronze capsule embedded in the ceiling. Their New Year's Eve party was forgotten as they quickly climbed a ladder and hastened to remove the bronze capsule buried in the crumbling clay roof covering the chamber where they were gathered. Opening the green-aged bronze container, they found fragments of several manuscripts written by a certain Abba Syah.

The local deputy of the Egyptian government took immediate possession of the ancient fragments, sending them to Cairo for translation. The manuscript pieces were carbon-dated as originating in the early fourth century of the Christian Era. The translation of one scroll fragment revealed that Abba Syah had been a Christian priest who, upon reaching old age, had abandoned his priestly duties to become a hermit. He came to the Coptic monks asking to live in a small hut on the roof of their monastery.

He spent the remaining years of his life in his one-room hermitage praying and meditating. Every third day the monks would kindly climb the ladder to his rooftop hut and leave a flask of water, a loaf of bread and a few vegetables outside the door.

The second manuscript fragment revealed that shortly after Abba Syah had taken up the life of a hermit, he also began to entertain visitors from heaven. He never called them apparitions or visions, but only visits. The first of these heavenly visitors was the Archangel Raphael, with whom the hermit discussed ordinary topics like the ailments that accompany advancing age. Several other archangels followed Raphael, but all these angelic visitors were only an advance team that prepared for the coming of the real visitor, the Risen Jesus.

The third and largest manuscript fragment recorded the frequent visits of the Risen Jesus, in which the two always shared a meal. Abba Syah recorded that on at least three occasions Jesus actually stayed overnight and slept in his hermitage. Their conversations were about prayer, the spiritual life and the puzzle of who God is — along with the sharing of jokes and funny stories. While Abba Syah spoke of these conversations, he did not record any of them.

The scroll fragments fortunately do contain Abba Syah's faithful recounting of what he calls "The Sayings of Jesus." Abba Syah always recorded these short parable-like remarks of Jesus in the present tense. Apparently, these sayings of Jesus were spoken during their dinner conversations. We are now privileged to be able to publish them for the first time in this small volume.

The Sayings of Jesus

"Don't believe in God," says Jesus, "follow God."
                    —Fragment 2, Syah Scroll, 5: 1

"The fastest way to get to heaven," says Jesus, "is to go through hell."
                    —Fragment 2, Syah Scroll, 5: 2

"Blessed are the poor," says Jesus, "who cleverly appear to be rich."
                    —Fragment 2, Syah Scroll, 5: 3

"God is allergic to crowds," says Jesus, "so get lost."
                    —Fragment 2, Syah Scroll, 5: 4

Publisher's Note:

As you can see, the "Sayings of Jesus" tend to be provocative, challenging and even unsettling, and so need to be properly pondered. To give you space and time to reflect upon them, the remaining sayings of the Abba Syah manuscript are scattered through the rest of the text of this book.

May you find each of our Lord's sayings to be like a rung on a ladder. Slowly climb one rung at a time, either upward or downward, pausing to get a solid feel of each rung before moving on to the next one.

As Abba Syah said, "Climb not the Holy Ladder in haste, lest you find yourself out on a limb."

The Letter-Notes
of Abba Syah

Several months after the team of archeologists discovered the first scrolls of Abba Syah, they made another wonderful discovery in the ruins of the same ancient Coptic monastery. In what had been the monastic library they found among the few ancient scrolls to survive one tattered manuscript bearing the title of *Abba Syah's Letter-Notes*.

These Letter-Notes are the written responses to questions left at the door of Abba Syah's rooftop hermitage hut by the brothers of the monastery. In the tradition of the Desert Fathers and Mothers he gave spiritual direction, and as a hermit his guidance was given by means of written messages.

The following responses are among the few Letter-Notes that survived. They are printed here through the kindness of the Egyptian government and the Museum of Antiquities in Cairo.

Dear Brother,

In your note detailing your struggles living in the monastery, you asked, "Is a monastic life the most perfect way to follow the Way and achieve holiness, or should I seek another walk of life?"

As regard to finding the right walk of life: For some, to live a religious life is "to walk on eggshells." On the other hand, to seek holiness in the midst of the world is "to walk a tightrope." Regardless of which way one chooses, to walk the Way with honesty is always "to walk the plank." If the Gospel's call to holiness cannot be lived in the marketplace and in every walk of life, then it's not truly Good News.

May God bless your walk,
with joy and hope,

Abba Syah

Dear Brother,

You wrote asking, "What is the vocation of a mystic?" It is not some rare call, since everyone who has fallen in love with God is called to be a mystic.

For now, I encourage you to be about the _work_ of a mystic. The Earth is encircled in a giant evil vine that is slowly choking it to death. This poisonous vine has 10,000 times 10,000 roots. These roots are deeply entwined in every church, mosque, synagogue and temple, in the capitals of all nations and places of business and commerce, large and small. One of these roots is also in your heart. That root is the source of all your selfishness, which further poisons the world.

With passion, dig away at this vine day by day, year by year, until you root it out. By means of this inner work, part of the evil vine dies! Yes, the vocation of a mystic first involves digging up one's own vine root. Being derooted, a mystic shares lavishly in God's love of the world and in Christ's redemption of the world — and so shines with the glory of God.

Yours joyfully, shovel in hand,

Abba Syah

P.S. Brother, I urge you to use the greatest of care in digging up your evil root. Growing alongside and often intertwined with it is your holy root, planted there by God. From this holy root grows all that is beautiful and wondrous in the world.

Dear Brother,

Your note asked about how one grows in humility. You wrote about your efforts to always sit in the very last seat in chapel, to deny that any work you have accomplished is good and to hold your hands over your ears so as not to hear any praise directed toward you. You say that you asked the abbot to put you in charge of cleaning the privy of the brothers — and that you have practiced other such debasing disciplines. You wrote, "Is this the correct way to grow in humility?"

No, brother, I'm afraid it's not! Such debasing actions only make you more self-conscious, more focused on yourself. If you truly seek to be humble, then always and everywhere put the needs and concerns of others before your own. Meditate on the words of Philippians (2:3): "Regard others and their needs and interests as more important than your own." I assure you, this will require far more discipline and patience and love than cleaning out the privy.

May God bless you, brother, for your kindness to me, and notwithstanding this note, may you continue to empty the chamber pot that I leave at my door.

In your service,

Abba Syah

Dear Brother,

Your note asked, "What should one most guard against when seeking to be Godlike?" You particularly inquired about sins against chastity and sloth — which the ancients often warned against.

Perhaps the best answer is: Guard against becoming a calculator! Being a calculating brother prevents you from being a spontaneous lover. As you know, Brother Treasurer, who's responsible for managing the limited funds of the monastery, uses the pebbles strung upon the cords of his abacus to carefully compute his sums. He uses his calculator as a tool to serve the community.

But those who constantly calculate the cost of loving, the cost of everything they invest in life, soon develop a calculating heart. Such heart-calculators have strings of soul stones — much like the kidney stones that afflict poor Brother Doorkeeper. These soul stones are painful, and persons so afflicted suffer sharp pains whenever they think they've given away more love than they've received. While only a few of us have kidney stones or gallstones, many suffer from soul stones.

Brother, when you love, which I hope is often, never view it as a returnable investment. Never calculate your love for God and others. Rather, as St. Paul says in his little-known letter to the Filipinos, "Throw love away as wildly as a sailor spends money on a shore leave in Manila."

Your drunken sailor on the roof,

Abba Syah

Dear Brother,

Thank you for your note and questions about the quest for holiness. I can understand your efforts to become holy through your strict adherence to daily times of communal prayer and through your devotions, fasting and various private acts of penance and self-denial. You had some doubt as to whether this is "the Way"? You also posed the question, "Why do those who dedicate their entire lives to prayer and religious life often not become holy?"

Instead of replying directly to your question, I'm enclosing part of a letter I received from my good friend Amma Ananda. She is a true desert mother who lives as a hermit in a cave about a mile from this monastery. Over the years she and I have exchanged letters. Some of the townsfolk who go to her for spiritual direction are kind enough to carry our letters back and forth. So, I am including the part of her letter that speaks to your problem.

In closing, I encourage you to be patient and ever alert, for the road to God is both long and short.

Your brother on the road,

Abba Syah

often in my thoughts and prayers. My life is so full in its emptiness. I will explain, dear friend.

At a recent Eucharist I celebrated with a few of my disciples, my homily was based on one of the stories of Jesus you sent me some time ago. It was the story of Jesus passing through a village, when a woman in the crowd cried out, "Holy are you, Jesus of Nazareth, for in you God has visited his people." Jesus replied to her, "Why do you call me holy? There is only One who is holy."

Later, one of his disciples asked, "Master, surely you are holy, are you not?"

And Jesus replied, "Why do you call me Master? Only God is our Lord and Master!"

At that none of his disciples dared ask him any more questions. However, Jesus was compassionate with them, and so he shed some light on his responses: "My friends, I understand your confusion, but it's important for you not to <u>mis</u>understand about holiness and the Way. You look at the work I do and the words I speak, and you say that I am holy. But you must know that I do not try to be holy! Rather, each day I only try to be hollow!"

Thank you, dear friend, for that story. It speaks so wonderfully to the process of becoming Godlike. It opened doors for my disciples into the mystery of hollowness. I shared with them the wisdom of daily trying to become hollow of one's self, hollow of wants and ambitions, of opinions and judgments, for this is the royal road to freedom. As you know so well, dear friend, only then can the Wind of God truly whistle through a soul, making the music of heaven.

I also told my disciples that when the angel came to Mary, the soon-to-be mother of Jesus, she was not full of grace! As you can guess, several were shocked. But I continued by saying that rather than being full of anything, Mary of Nazareth was hollow of everything! It was thus that the Holy Mother attained true virginity. I left those spiritual seekers entrusted to my care with an image, saying that the way to become Godlike is the same way that musical flutes are made — that is, by being hollowed out.

Ah, dear friend, if only spiritual seekers would stop filling up their lives with all those religious exercises that so easily bloat egos and

Publisher's Note:

This fragment is all that remains of Amma Ananda's letter that Abba Syah enclosed in his note to the brother.

It is noteworthy that the discovery of this Letter-Note inspired archeologists to search for the hermitage cave of the Desert Mother, Amma Ananda. The story of that important exploration is detailed in the next chapter.

The Tradition of the Desert Fathers and Mothers

Some three hundred years after the first Pentecost, the infant Christian church and the whole world were caught up in enormous social change and turmoil. The previously persecuted Christians were now basking in the warm glow of Emperor Constantine's blessing. Membership in the faith expanded quickly, and the young church grew fat in prosperity as a new partner of the Imperial Establishment.

As all this was happening, a new movement appeared in Christianity. It began as an exodus by a few men and women to the deserts of Egypt and Palestine, where they could live a radical Christian lifestyle. They sought to live the original, unedited life of a disciple of Jesus. They desired to practice a religion naked of the Roman compromises with Constantine's Court. In order to survive in the hostile conditions of the desert, these spiritual seekers began to gather in small, structureless groups, which orbited around a single man or woman known for his or her holiness. These early spiritual magnets, who later became know as Desert Fathers and Mothers, were given titles of great respect by their disciples: *Abba* (father) or *Amma* (mother).

These small communities balanced the rare gifts of the freedom required for solitude and personal prayer with the discipline required for an ongoing reformation of life. A disciple with a spiritual problem would come to an Amma or Abba seeking guidance and wisdom. These guides would often offer a parable-story or brief saying to help the disciples with their problems. Later, these replies to disciples were written down as the Wisdom Sayings of the Desert.

The Sayings and Stories
of Amma Ananda

Shortly after the discovery in Egypt of Abba Syah's lost scrolls, a manuscript of a certain Amma Ananda was unearthed. References in Abba Syah's Letter-Notes led to the Desert Mother's hermitage cave some distance from the ruins of Abba Syah's

29

ancient Coptic monastery. Sometime during the sixth century, a landslide had sealed the entrance to Amma Ananda's cave dwelling. The archeologists who dug through the rockslide were fascinated by the simple yet artistic beauty of her dwelling. But their greatest find was a hidden lower cave at the rear of Amma's hermitage. Using a ladder they descended into that lower cave and discovered a small chapel with an altar set in the wall. Above the altar was a carved icon of St. Mary Magdalene. Pottery shards and other artifacts in the chapel clearly indicated that Amma Ananda herself had been the celebrant of the Supper of the Lord, the Eucharist.

Amma Ananda's former Roman name remains unknown, and today scholars are divided about how she came by her unusual Sanskrit name, *Ananda*, which means *bliss*. Hindu and Buddhist monks from India were known to have traveled along the trade roads that snaked their way from the East to Egypt. Some scholars believe she may have encountered some of these Eastern monks while in the Egyptian city of Alexandria on her way to the desert. In the ancient world, Alexandria was renowned for its great library and its warm acceptance of diverse religious and philosophical ideas.

Some of the sayings of Mother Bliss, Amma Ananda, are printed here through the kindness of the Egyptian Antiquities Museum in Cairo. The author and the publisher express a special debt of gratitude to the museum's staff and to Dr. Ishtiaq Nasr Hossein for their invaluable assistance.

The Sayings
of Amma Ananda

Publisher's Note:

Only a few fragments remain of the rich sayings of this Desert Mother:

"Blessed are the poor, the truly poor, who have in this life given up all heavenly rewards."

"Blessed are those who enjoy Paradise here and now, and look upon the face of God in every place and at every moment, for theirs is the reign of God."

"The heart is a potbellied stove. Throw in more logs today than yesterday, and more logs tomorrow than you did today. Strive to love God more each day of your life, until you become a raging fire."

"The most impure thoughts that you must purge from your mind are not about sex. Be more concerned about thoughts of being superior to others and thoughts that divide you from others."

"Fear not particular friendships. Fear, instead, not having any true friendships, for they are icons of intimacy with the Beloved."

"The last stage of poverty is to give up poverty."

The Stories
of Amma Ananda

Editor's Note:

It was the tradition of fourth and fifth century pilgrims who came to the remote hermitages of the Desert Fathers and Mothers to greet the holy one by saying, "Please, give me a word by which to live."

A Word by Which to Live

A pilgrim came to Amma Ananda requesting a word by which to live. Amma gave her the word "Ah." The seeker pronounced that simple syllable, and in a flash her heart opened to the wonder at the heart of life. The pilgrim walked away repeating the word, sensing awe in even the most commonplace wonders she passed along the way.

To another pilgrim, Amma said, "You're lucky! Today, you get a bonus, for I'm giving you two words: *thank you*."

The pilgrim was disappointed and said, "Amma, did I come all this way to be given so common an expression? How can this everyday phrase be a word of life?"

She answered him, "I assure you, if you make *thank you* your constant prayer word, you will find life in great abundance."

To one particularly creative and adventurous pilgrim who had made a long and arduous journey to the hermit's cave, Amma Ananda gave a small leather box, saying, "Here is a special 'word' for you." The pilgrim opened the small box and to her surprise found inside the twenty-six letters of the alphabet. Amma responded to the astonished look on the pilgrim's face by saying, "With this tool kit the Word can inspire you to form just the right word for every life situation."

Amma's response to another pilgrim's request for a word was simply to sit in silence. After about half an hour the pilgrim complained, "Amma, I have traveled a great distance earnestly desiring to hear from you a word by which to live, yet you say nothing!" As the disgruntled pilgrim rose to leave, Amma took a piece of paper and wrote on it. Then she folded the paper and handed it to the pilgrim. He unfolded the paper and read the message, "Silence will teach you how to live." The pilgrim silently bowed to Amma and left the cave.

Zen masters were known to give such silent koans that communicated essential life messages without the use of words. Naturally, no book can contain such "words" by which to gain enlightenment, yet stories and parables can point to an understanding of these silent words. One story is told of a multitude that had assembled to hear the Buddha give a sermon on the Dharma, the Way. The Buddha, however, only sat silently and then held up a flower. Finally, one disciple, with only a smile, announced his comprehension of Buddha's teaching.

A Christian Desert Father said, "To live without speaking is better than to speak without living."

The Most Frightening Words

"Amma Ananda," asked a disciple, "of all the words of Jesus, which do you think the church today would find most frightening?"

Amma replied, "His words in Nazareth, 'I have come to set the prisoners free.'"

"Prisoners?" asked the disciple.

"Yes," she answered, "true disciples of Jesus must not be prisoners of fear, guilt or shame. Nor should they be held bound by church laws that are made greater than, or even equal in value to, the commands of Christ."

The Taste of God

A disciple came to Amma complaining that he had failed to find God in his spiritual exercises. "Teacher, I pray the psalms seven times a day. I fast completely from food and water three times a week. I meditate daily for three hours, and I am chaste as the Mother of God. But, sadly, in all of these, I do not experience God!"

Amma Ananda slowly shook her head and said, "In these holy exercises you do not taste God? Indeed, learned men teach us that since Adam's sin we live in a valley of tears, and only in the next life will we experience God."

"But you, Amma, what do you say? I trust your wisdom."

"If you really want to taste God in your spiritual exercises, you might try to have fun!"

"Fun?" the shocked disciple asked.

"Yes, unless we find joy in all we do, how can we taste God? As St. Paul said, 'Rejoice always!'[1] So, go home and have some fun!"

Fun is only a folk term for rejoicing. When we've really enjoyed Mass or a time of prayer, why not say, "I had fun!" Having fun in worship is giving the highest possible compliment, since God is Joy.

[1] 1 Thessalonians 5: 16

Patting the Goat

One day, a disciple came to Amma Ananda and asked, "Teacher, I seek perfection and strive daily to avoid all sins of sex, greed, gluttony and anger. Tell me, what is the most dangerous sin?"

Amma said, "Let me tell you the story of Adam's confession:

One day after he had left home in Eden's garden, Adam knelt and looked heavenward and confessed to God. "Bless me, Father, for I have sinned," he said, tears running down his cheeks. "I realize now that after Eve and I ate the apple, I passed the buck. Not only did I disobey you, but I made excuses for my sin and blamed Eve."

For a long time the response from heaven was silence. Then, a solitary cloud drifted across the blue sky, and from it came a voice, "You passed the buck? Don't you mean you patted the goat?" asked God. "You put your sin on the nearest scapegoat you could find. The sin that wearies me the most is when my children refuse to be responsible for their lives and behavior. You will never grow up, Adam, you will never become mature, unless you stop patting the goat. Stand up, my son, your sins are forgiven. Now, go in peace and do not pat the goat again."

The Quest for Greatness

"Amma," asked a disciple, "I seek to be perfect, so would you help show me how can I uncover my weaknesses?"

"That is an excellent question for a true seeker," Amma Ananda replied, "since the unenlightened usually pretend they don't have any weaknesses. What have you discovered so far by your exploration of your weaker side?"

"I find," the disciple eagerly confessed, "that I am impatient with others. I also postpone decisions and tasks I find unpleasant as long as possible. Moreover, I am prejudiced toward various kinds of people. Yet, these are only my obvious weaknesses."

"Are those your weaknesses, or are they the results of your weaknesses?" she asked.

Confused, the student fumbled out a question, "Well, then, Amma, how do I find my real weaknesses?"

Amma Ananda paused and smiled, "If you are truly serious about finding them, go home and write out a list of all your strengths. For you will then also have a list of your weaknesses!"

The Fortunate
Fortune Hunters

"Amma," asked a disciple, "how does one find the reign of God?"

"Fortunate, indeed, are those who find the reign of God," Amma Ananda said. "It is like a man and woman who stumbled upon a hidden treasure secretly buried in a field. They quickly covered the hiding place with rocks, ran home and sold everything — I mean everything — they owned to purchase that field. Then they returned to the field, dug up the treasure and possessed a great fortune."[1]

"Yes, but how do we know," asked the skeptical disciple, "that they found God's kingdom?"

"That's easy," Amma replied, "because they immediately went out and gave away all their new fortune to the poor!"

"Amma," asked her disciple, "didn't you say they had sold everything they owned to buy the field? So, if they gave away all their newly found fortune, they would be penniless!"

"Yes," smiled Amma Ananda, "weren't they fortunate — blessed beyond measure?"

[1] See Matthew 13: 44

Living with God

A disciple came to Amma Ananda and asked, "I want to constantly live in the presence of God. Teacher, how do I do this?"

"Become a cliff dweller," she said.

"Amma, there are some cliffs in a canyon many miles from here. Is that where I should go to live with God?"

"No," she answered, "the cliff where you are to dwell is as close as your shadow. Go, daily live there on the edge of the grand canyon."

"You mean *the* Grand Canyon?"

"No, this canyon is not limited by geography. You will find the truly grand canyon of danger and delight whenever you live on the edge, whenever you are out of control and not in charge, and must simply trust. Dwell as close as possible to the edge of that fearfully deep canyon and you will live infinitely close to God."

The following parables and stories
were composed in the living tradition
of Abba Syah and Amma Ananda
and the Desert Fathers and Mothers.

Preface Parable

Up or Down the Ladder

"Teacher," asked the student, "is the Way we are to follow best understood as a life-pilgrimage?"

"For some, perhaps," replied the teacher with a smile, "but for me the Way is more like a ladder that I must use daily."

The student beamed, "I understand! It's as the spiritual books tell us: Prayer is raising the mind and heart to God. The ladder of which you speak, then, is the way we must climb up to heaven?"

"Well, yes and no. Indeed, at times a ladder is needed to ascend above the noisy surface of daily life in order to encounter the Divine Mystery of Love. At other times," he said with a grin that showed all his teeth, "in fact, more often, you must climb down deeply into the guts of daily life in order to find God. Since religions are so oriented to the otherworldly, descending into daily reality is far more difficult than ascending."

To the student's surprise, the teacher went on, "Religion prefers to be like a visitor from outer space, since it finds the sensual world such a threat to the spiritual." The student's surprise was somersaulted into shock as the teacher laughed and continued, "Ah, yes, to find God you must descend into the nitty-gritty, the realm of the nits and tiny lice! I assure you, the Holy, Happy Creator is as present in the nits that are crawling around in your hair as in the billions of cosmic galaxies."

The stunned student's lips silently formed the word "nits" as the teacher held up a long index finger, a clear sign to the student that it was time for a story.

The Quest
for the Burning Bush

The ecumenical expedition composed of Christians of various denominations, as well as Jewish and Muslim scholars, met in Cairo where they held a joint press conference. Before an array of television cameras the expedition's leaders announced their intention to find the famed burning bush of Moses.

A reporter asked, "Do you believe that after more than three thousand years the burning bush still exists?" The spokesperson for the group, Italian Jesuit Father Santiago Santianno, replied, "Why else would such learned men as these be on their way to Mount Horeb in the Sinai?"

"And," added a bearded Jewish scholar, "our hope is that just as God gave a message to Moses about the future, the Holy One might perhaps use the bush again to speak to us at this critical time in history."

The expedition flew by private plane to the tip of the Sinai desert and from there embarked at once for Mount Horeb. The scholars painstakingly examined every single bush, large and small, as they made their way to the holy mount Horeb, reasoning that it might have been near and not on Horeb itself that God appeared to Moses. Gathered around the cooking fire of their evening camps, the scholars discussed what a great blessing to the world's three great religions it would be to find the sacred burning bush. "A shrine," declared an enthusiastic Islamic scholar, "it would be a grand common shrine to which all our peoples could come on pilgrimage."

The Horeb ecumenical expedition lasted over three years and cost millions of dollars, an expense subsidized mainly by the donations of a couple of religiously very conservative billionaires in America. Yet, while the scholars examined thousands of desert bushes, none was found to emit even a few sparks or show any signs of being divinely charred. They listened carefully to the branches on every bush, but no one heard the voice of God, or any voices. No press conference was held when they prepared to make their defeated departure for home from the desert of Horeb.

At the very same hour the expedition members were boarding their plane in the Sinai, near Milesville, South Dakota, a farmer's wife was in her kitchen doing the dishes when her dish towel exploded into flames. Out of the flaming towel came a voice, "Mara, Mara, remove your slippers for the place where you stand is holy ground."

*"**Entrée las pucheras anda el Senor**," said the great Spanish mystic St. Teresa of Avila: "God strolls amidst the pots and pans."*

The Problem with Religion

"Teacher," said the disciple, "we all know you have problems with organized religion. Why is this?"

"What you say is not entirely true," the teacher responded. "What I dislike about religion is that it's uppity."

"Yes, I agree that religions can be arrogant and haughty," answered another disciple, "and so can become self-righteous."

"That's not what I mean by being uppity," replied the teacher. "Rather, it's that religion is uplifting!" The stunned disciples sat corralled in confusion.

"When religious people pray to God," the teacher continued, "they look up. Churches are built with upward sweeping lines and with tall steeples that point up to the skies. Yet God is not up or down, and God is both up and down. Moreover, to seek God, the primary direction is neither up nor down, but *in*!"

The Lord Buddha said, "The way is not in the sky, the way is in the heart."[1]

"The Church is large," says Jesus, "but the Kingdom is small."
—Fragment 2, Syah Scroll, 5: 11

[1] The *Dhammapada*, The Sayings of the Buddha

No Homecoming

"Teacher," asked the student, "I have a problem with the seeming harshness of God in the Garden of Eden. Jesus says we are to forgive seven times seventy; why didn't God forgive Adam and Eve when they sinned? The Bible says God not only drove them out of the garden but stationed an angel with a flaming sword at the gates to prevent them from ever coming home again. Please, teacher, speak to me about this."

After a pause, the teacher said, "It teaches a most important lesson of life that few wish to learn: You can never go home again."

For millenniums the story of Adam and Eve has sadly had a narrow religious interpretation. As a Biblical parable, might you turn it inside out and play with other possible meanings? For starters, have you ever found an angel with a flaming sword blocking your return to an earlier, more innocent age?

"Tomorrow will not be today," says Jesus, "so learn to enjoy change."
—Fragment 2, Syah Scroll, 5: 18

If the Shoe Fits

The road to the great shrine of the saint's tomb, known for its many miracle-rich relics, was crowded with pilgrims. Among the pilgrims traveling to the shrine was a teacher and his student. The two walked along mostly in prayerful silence, since the teacher taught that the road to every shrine is itself a shrine. Suddenly, the silence of the road was broken — from behind them came loud sounds of *slap, slap, slap*.

Without turning around to look, the teacher said, "Quickly, let's move off to the side to let the holy friars pass." They stood at the edge of the road, making way for a large band of friars wearing flowing habits and sandals that were far too large for their feet.

Even before the last friar had passed by, there followed a thunderous *flap, flap, flap*, accompanied by an equally loud *tap, tap, tap*. The student quickly turned to see who was coming, while the teacher stood with his eyes closed. Groups of various orders of monks followed by various orders of nuns walked past, raising clouds of dust with their *flap-flap, tap-tapping*. When the dust cleared, the teacher opened his eyes and smiled, "Come, let us continue our pilgrimage."

"Teacher," asked the student, "why did the groups of friars, monks and nuns all wear shoes so large that they had difficulty walking in them? Their sandals were big enough for giants."

"Those were shoes of giants," replied the teacher, "and the noise we heard was due to the fact that the feet wearing them weren't big enough! For if you want to grow large feet, you must live a true holy poverty."

"I don't understand, Teacher," said the student, "all who passed by have taken a holy vow of poverty. They've given up all personal wealth and renounced the world. Haven't they forsaken everything?"

"Ah, for the most part," replied the teacher, "they've only traded what God had loaned them in exchange for a life of relative comfort, security and respectability!"

The two walked in silence for a while, until the student asked, "How does that explain why their shoes and sandals were so large?"

"It is the tradition in religious communities," the teacher answered, "to dress like the holy founder, but their founders were all giants!"

The student looked down at the sandals of the teacher, who noticed his glance and said, "If the shoe fits, wear it!"

Like members of many religions, the friars, monks and nuns in this parable are followers of a holy founder. Yet, in the case of Christians, more than Baptism is required to follow in Jesus' footsteps. We must grow larger feet.

Jesus invited a certain rich young man who was eager to become his follower: "Go home and sell all you own and give it to the poor, and then come and follow me."[1] Yet, Jesus calls each of us who wants to be his follower to a more radical kind of poverty than simply returning to God what has only been loaned to us. It is the radical poverty of discipleship that grows feet large enough to walk in his giant footprints. The poverty that enlarges both feet and soul is found in his invitation to the cross: "You must deny your very self...."[2] We need to ask: Why doesn't a religious way of life startle us to greatness any more?

[1] Matthew 19: 21
[2] Matthew 16: 24

The Ladder

It was the ninth hour as the sky turned an ugly black, the three criminals hanging in agony on their crosses of death. As the wind began to swirl brown clouds of dust around the hilltop, a Roman soldier, moved by pity, soaked a sponge in drugged wine, placed it on the end of his lance and offered it to the dying men.

The first dying criminal raised his head and eagerly sucked at the sponge. Finished, he threw his head backwards, gasping for air. The soldier next came to the criminal hanging in the middle and raised the sponge on his spear to him. Without raising his battered head, he only shook it in a wordless "no." The soldier pushed the sponge closer, "Take it, take it! There's no shame in trying to dull the pain." The condemned man simply shook his head again and spoke a few faint words.

"I can't hear you," shouted the soldier. "If you don't want the drugged wine, what do you want?"

Raising his head, the dying man opened his parched lips, "Give me a ladder." Hearing this, the other soldiers burst out in laughter, "He wants to climb down from his cross!"

The dying criminal shook his head, saying, "I don't want to climb down. I want to climb higher."

Grabbing the large wooden ladder used to raise prisoners to their crosses, another soldier jeered at the crucified criminal, "Anything we can do to please you." He began slamming the heavy ladder again and again against the already bruised and bloody body of the dying man.

The other soldiers danced around his cross, chanting, "Climb higher, Your Majesty, for as the King of the Criminals you must hang higher than common criminals." The soldiers continued to ridicule their dying victim and to slam the ladder against him. He only cried out, "I find my joy in God my Savior, for the Almighty has done great things for me."

The criminal crucified on his left yelled down at those below, "Stop abusing this man, for he is a son of God."

The criminal on the far right yelled over, "Shut your mouth, fool, this is no business of ours."

Then, the one crucified in the middle slowly turned his head to the one on his left, saying, "I rejoice that you also have used the ladder. I assure you, this very day you are with me in Paradise."[1]

Along with the spear, nails and crown of thorns, the ladder is a primary passion symbol. It thus belongs among the mystical devices of exploration and navigation for those who are God-seekers.

*From the Latin root **trans scandere**, the word transcendent literally means "to climb above." To transcend the gravity of the heavy-laden world of suffering requires rising above the physical pain of the moment. Such an ascension is based on a faith that God joins Easter victories to our Good Friday agonies. To find joy not only in a beautiful sunset or serene forest setting but even in life's pains, suffering and difficulties, requires climbing above the surface of these experiences in order to find the source of joy, who is in all.*

[1] See Luke 23: 43

How You Fold It

A student came upon the teacher while he was reading the local newspaper. The student patiently waited for him to lower the paper and speak to him, but the teacher seemed oblivious to his presence. The student loudly cleared his throat, but the teacher continued reading. Finally, the student interjected, "Teacher, excuse me for bothering you, but I have come seeking wisdom. Would you please tell me a parable?"

Without lowering the newspaper, the teacher replied, "Life is full of parables. Like the one here on the front page. Let me read you this parable, and then you can go and ponder its meaning."

"But teacher," objected the student, "it appears you're reading from an inside page of the paper, not the front page."

"Which page is in front," replied the teacher, folding the newspaper inside out, "all depends on how you fold it."

Front Page Parable

Choose the Right Ladder

"This is a good parable," said the teacher. "It's a news article about recommendations made by the American Academy of Orthopedic Surgeons of Rosemont, Illinois. The physicians are concerned, the article says, about the improper use of ladders."

The teacher smiled a large grin and continued, "For a ladder climber like yourself it holds much wisdom, since it says that more than half a million people are sent to emergency rooms or doctor's offices because of falls from ladders! The orthopedic academy urges people always to use ladders of the proper length. If you're climbing indoors, for instance, use a stepladder or step stool, and if you're climbing outdoors use a taller ladder. Moreover, the physicians urge always inspecting the ladder before using it."

"If that's a parable," asked the bewildered student, "what is it about?"

"Don't use a step stool to reach heaven," said the teacher.

The Three Most Encouraging Words of Jesus

A group of students sat around their teacher when one of them, wishing to test him, asked, "Teacher, what are the three most encouraging words of Jesus?"

"His three words on the cross," the teacher answered immediately: 'It is finished.'" Then the teacher rose to leave the room.

"You confuse us, Teacher," said the student. "You cannot leave us with such a mystery. Why are those words in any way encouraging?"

"Because those words tell you that it takes a lifetime to achieve your spiritual destiny!"

Today people are in a hurry, even to become holy. The most important wedding of virtues in the quest for holiness is the marriage of patience to passion. Seekers rarely have both the perpetual passion to be Godlike and the patience to wait a lifetime to achieve their goal. Both qualities are learned in the shadow of the ladder of the cross. As St. Bernard of Clairvaux, the great spiritual giant of the twelfth century, said, "Either you must go up or you must come down, you inevitably fall if you try to stand still. It is certain the man (woman) who does not try to be better is not even good; when you stop trying to be better, then you cease to be good."

"No artist fully develops his or her gift," says Jesus, "so never cease being both the student and teacher."
—Fragment 2, Syah Scroll, 5: 23

In

last year's

nest

there

are

no

eggs

this year.

The Tale of Two Bells

Once, long ago, the bell in the village church tower was visiting with the pigeons in the belfry about its work as a holy pealer. "I was consecrated with holy oil by the bishop to do holy work," the bell said proudly. "When it's time to call the people to doing good, I ring out for all to hear. I peal to the villagers to be generous to the poor and to pray. Even now," said the bell, "I see by the tower clock that it's time to ring out the call to prayer," and the bell tolled loudly. Indeed, the church bell also clanged loudly whenever it was accidentally struck by an unkind word, a missed appointment or when someone was rude to it.

One day, a wandering old mendicant bell from the Orient came passing through the village and sat down to rest on the church steps. The church bell looked down and, seeing this as an opportunity to take a day off, called down to the old bell on the steps, "Say, stranger, would you mind taking over my duties for a day or two so I can go on a little holiday?"

The wandering mendicant bell looked up to the top of the belfry and with some hesitation asked, "Well, what would my duties be?"

"Nothing difficult," answered the consecrated bell. "You just have to ring out the times of prayer and worship. Also, you can peal out a little homily to the people on the need to be good. Nothing long, mind you. Here, let me show you." And the church bell clanged out a brief message.

The old mendicant bell agreed to the request, and the consecrated bell quickly packed an overnight bag and happily skipped out of town.

When the next hour of prayer came, the old mendicant bell beautifully rang out the call to prayer. All the villagers stopped in the middle of whatever they were doing, held fast by the awesome clarity of the chiming bell. Then a wondrous thing happened: One and all bowed their heads and prayed — even the unbelievers! On Sunday, the visiting bell pealed out melodious prayers and then chimed out a homily. The resonance of its heavenly pealing drifted out over the village, across the fields and forest, causing even the birds and animals to pause and listen. The bell's haunting homily echoed for days in the villagers' ears.

A few days later, the consecrated bell returned and was met at the town gate by a crowd of people who couldn't stop talking about how wonderful was the beautiful chiming of the visiting bell. The church bell was filled with envy and clanged loudly as it climbed up the flight of steps leading to the top of the bell tower.

Frightened flapping pigeons flew in all directions as the church bell shouted, "Get out of *my* church tower!" Then, with all the force it could muster, the church bell gave the mendicant bell a mighty blow. But from the old wandering bell came a melodic pealing of such unbelievable beauty as to cause everyone in the village to become transfixed statue-like by the awesome tones. Ashamed by the beauty of the old bell's sound, the church bell asked, "How can you respond so graciously when struck in anger?"

Slowly climbing down the tower steps, the old mendicant bell replied, "When struck, the sound produced comes from the metal of which one is made."

Hurrying behind, the church bell said, "Naturally, but I'm not made of fine bronze as are you."

The old mendicant bell slowly turned and said,

"Friend, just like you, I was made of common brass with all its impurities, but the metal in my bell has been purified countless times by the refiner's fire, until now it is finely tempered bronze."

As the old wandering bell departed through the town gate, the consecrated church bell sadly shook its head, for it had a great dread of the refiner's fire.

Daily life has more than enough opportunities to be purified, if we are willing to lovingly enter the Holy Refiner's furnace. When all of life is embraced with love, daily pains become opportunities for purification, enhancing our inner beauty.

If we use the ascending, descending ladder of daily spiritual growth, this Valley of Tears is transformed into the Mount of the Transfiguration. Using your ladder patiently and prayerfully day by day, it is possible to spontaneously respond in a sacred way to every situation in life, even to rudeness and injury.

So, when you suddenly feel the hot blast from the opening door of the Refiner's furnace, do not run away!

The Rare True Friend

One day a student asked, "Teacher, as everyone knows, there are friends — and, then, there are friends. Tell me, what is a true friend?"

"A true friend," answered the teacher with a smile, "is the one with whom you can go skinny-dipping."

"Teacher," said the surprised student, "I don't understand. Why is swimming nude with another a sign of true friendship?"

"Because," replied the teacher, "the love of real friendship allows one to bare all. True friendship is not a costume party or masked ball."

"But who is able to take the risk of still being loved after having so completely exposed oneself to another?" asked the student.

"Very few," the teacher replied sadly. "Very few, indeed, are willing to take such a great risk."

"Those who've never been in love," says Jesus, "at the Wedding Feast will find themselves naked."
—Fragment 2, Syah Scroll, 5: 20

The Man with the Really Good Eye

The man with the really good eye arrived one day on a bus carrying only a few meager possessions. From that day onward, he'd always look deeply into the face of whomever he met, man or woman, old or young, and declare, "Beau-T-full," his voice rising to place emphasis on the "T." Usually only babies and some women are called beautiful, yet he used this term to describe all kinds of people, as well as animals, flowers, trees and, in fact, most everything.

Whenever challenged on what basis he could make such a declaration, especially about persons and things that seemed anything but beautiful, he would just pat his pants pocket and reply with authority, "Like any doctor, I've got a license to practice, and it's right here in my pocket."

He never showed this license to anyone, and whenever he spoke of it he would quickly add, "And I'm practicing daily so I can become a great artist in my profession." When asked what was necessary to become great in his profession, he'd always answer, "Practice, practice, practice and a really good eye." And, if someone asked what kind of work he was licensed to do, he would grin and say, "Only a blind person would have to ask that question."

His response about the need for "a really good eye" might explain why he never merely glanced at anybody. Rather, he'd always pause to look deeply into every face and object. While some thought his intense look bordered on staring, it was more like an art critic's careful examination of a rare artpiece. Apparently, however, he never found any defects or imperfections, for after a few moments of intense inspection, he would always declare, "Beau-T-full!" Invariably, months or years of his repeated pronouncements had the effect of causing those around him, even men, to begin to see themselves as beautiful.

Some townsfolk slandered him, suggesting that anyone who sees others as beautiful must also see them as desirable, and so he must be some kind of pervert — a threat to the town and its children. The majority, however, simply considered him a harmless eccentric, and so no action was taken against him.

Whenever the man with the really good eye would meet someone on the street who had called him a pervert behind his back, he would stop and take more time than usual to look at that person. After looking intently into the slanderer's face, he would smile and declare, "Beau-T-full," and then continue walking down the street.

If asked how he could call those who had spoken ill of him "Beau-T-full," his reply would be, "With a really good eye you can see beneath the surface imperfections of any work of art. You can see what exists even beneath the stain of sin."

When the man died, the undertaker's first act was to search in his pants pocket for the mysterious license of which he had been so proud. Because he had not belonged to any church, his burial service was held in the funeral home chapel. An overflowing crowd of mourners nodded in agreement when the minister spoke of him as "a man who saw with God's eyes."

As a soloist sang a pious hymn, the undertaker, who was standing in the rear of the chapel, removed from his inside coat pocket the crumbled paper he had taken out of the dead man's pants pocket. He carefully unfolded the old, yellowed document and smiled as he looked at the state license for a beautician.

The prophet Samuel said, *"Not as humans see does God see, because humans see the appearance, but God looks into the heart."[1] Jesus admonished us, "Let those with eyes see...,"[2] to which could be added: ...to see with the eyes of God.*

The Divine Lover looks beneath surface appearances and sees the unbelievable beauty of each person and being. Such seeing is a mystical mirror vision, since the Divine Mystery is beholding its own awesome beauty reflected back from each heart. When we see with God's eyes, we become true beauticians who make persons and things beautiful merely by seeing them clearly.

The world and all who dwell within it can be divided into ugly or beautiful, plain or extraordinary, disgusting or appealing, only if you see with human eyes. "When people see some things as beautiful, other things become ugly.... Can you cleanse your inner vision until you see nothing but the light?"[3]

[1] 1 Samuel 16: 7
[2] See Matthew 13: 9-17
[3] *Tao Te Ching*, Chapters 2, 10

The New Parish Church

Two disciples invited their teacher to accompany them as they visited a brand new parish church built in the wealthy section of a nearby city. The large, gleaming stone structure had cost six million dollars and had taken over two years to build.

The disciples spoke in hushed voices of awe as they walked down the long main aisle, viewing the beautiful new oak pews, the impressive stone altar, the carved sanctuary furniture and large pulpit. The teacher silently gazed around at the church's artworks and its glowing stained glass windows. After spending a few minutes in prayer, the three left the church and began walking home. They walked in silence until the disciples, eager for the teacher's impression of the new church, asked, "Wasn't that a beautiful church?"

"Yes."

"Teacher, what about it impressed you the most?"

"That it's completely finished! Isn't that sad?"

The great medieval cathedrals took several centuries to complete. Parishioners were baptized, married and buried in their unfinished churches, usually worshipping their entire lives under scaffolding. Indeed, the stained glass windows were visual textbooks of the faith for the majority of people, who could neither read nor write. Yet it was the unfinished sacred places themselves that taught perhaps the most valuable lessons: that becoming church is a long, long process — that becoming a Christian is a long, long process which is completed only at one's wake.

The question that any worship space asks is, "What lesson does this sacred place teach?"

The Lamb

One afternoon a flock of gentle sheep was grazing leisurely when the lookout sheep cried out, "Look, the priest from the temple is coming to visit again!" All the sheep raised their heads to look at the distant approaching figure. Several of the older sheep quickly exchanged fearful glances with one another and then just as quickly smiled as their little lambs joyfully cried out, "The priest, the priest is coming to visit!"

When he reached the flock, the venerable holy man spread wide his arms in a greeting, "My little lambs, you are so beautiful and pure. Ah, my little ones, you are so precious, so precious." As the little lambs jubilantly crowded around the priest, each one eager for his personal attention, the greedy, wolflike eyes of the priest carefully examined each of them.

He reached down and picked up one of them. "So pure, so innocent, are you, my dear one," he said as he stroked its soft white wool. "You don't have a single blemish — you're perfect!" The little lamb's eyes grew large with gratitude and admiration for the priest. The lamb's playmates regretted their small blemishes, secretly wishing to be perfect so the priest would single them out for his praise and attention.

"Yes, my little one, you and I shall go home together," the priest said as he placed the lamb around his shoulders. The little lambs not chosen became bloated with jealousy as the priest departed with the small lamb. The parents of the chosen lamb, however, were grief-stricken. Yet, they were powerless to prevent him from carrying off their child. Several elderly sheep knew their pain, since on previous visits the temple priest had selected a young lamb child of theirs and taken it away.

Grief drained all life from the lamb's parents as the priest, with their young child on his shoulders, disappeared over the top ridge of the hill. A great storm of anger and rage howled in their hearts at being unable to prevent what had happened. An elder sheep tried to comfort them. "Chosen," said the old sheep, "in your pain know that your child was chosen."

In one voice the parents gasped, "Chosen?"

When small children and the innocent suffer, whether by personal tragedies or by acts of genocide or war, we are forced to ask: Is a great Mystery present? As horrible as it is to contemplate, in ancient Israel and most religious traditions, the innocent — those spotless, without blemish — have been chosen to suffer in order to redeem the many.

What about sexual and physical abuse of innocents? Is that a part of the Mystery in which one person, out of love, becomes a substitute for others — like the Lamb of God, Jesus, on the cross? Or, because that child has no freedom of choice, as Christ did, is this a perverse, twisted theology of redemption?

"When you hear hounds," says Jesus, "the hunters can't be far behind."
—Fragment 2, Syah Scroll, 5: 24

The Almost Empty Matchbox

To what shall I compare the kingdom of God today? It's like a brightly colored box of wooden matches which was almost empty.

One night when most of the remaining matches were fast asleep, three of them were quietly visiting with each other. "It's getting kind'a spooky in here," said the first match, "what with so many of our friends gone and no new ones coming to join us."

"More than spooky," replied the second match. "This place is getting the feel and look of a nursing home! Look around! Those of us who are left all have gray hair."

"You're only as old as you feel," the third match chirped happily.

To this the first match replied, "I'm not feeling old! I'm feeling lonely — especially with so few of us left on duty in here."

"Don't be depressed," replied the third match. "There are new young recruits coming to join us and our work. Not as many as before, true, but our heroic life still has great magnetic appeal. You just wait and see; things will change soon. It'll be just like the good old days!"

"From what I've seen of them new matches," replied the second match, "there aren't any real hotheads among them. They're just red caps, stick matches with big heads who enjoy hero status."

"Yeah," said the first match, "I say that you've got to *want* to burn if you feel you're called to be an incinerator. Few of those who have joined recently appear eager to burn themselves up for the cause."

"Well, I'm not all that eager to be called on either," said the second match, "at least not like I was when I first joined up. I'm hoping to get to retirement before I'm called on to go up in smoke."

"Retire!" snapped the third match. "How can you call yourself an incinerator and still talk about retirement? Especially when there are so few of us left? As for me, I signed on for life. Who could retire at a time like this?"

"Shush, you guys — be quiet," whispered the first match. "Hear that? The box is being opened, and you know what that means. One of us is going to be chosen." The three matches huddled as close as possible to one another with their eyes closed — praying.

"When you pray," says Jesus, "never ever say, 'Amen'!"

—Fragment 2, Syah Scroll, 5: 10

Prison-Pent

As a tiny baby the prisoner had been left in a basket on the doorstep of the prison. Perhaps his parents believed that only in prison would their child be safe from harm, fed three good meals a day and so be able to survive in a world as dangerous as this one.

The prisoner grew up enjoying his prison life, not having known any other. Yet his enjoyment of being incarcerated is remarkable in light of the fact that he was imprisoned in an AMF, an Absolute Maximum Facility, and was kept in complete solitary confinement twenty-four hours a day. Even his hour of exercise had to be taken completely alone in a small, enclosed athletic room.

The unique design of this maximum-security prison made it almost impossible for a child to know that he or she was actually inside a prison and almost as difficult to discover the existence of other prisoners. In his late teens, the prisoner became aware of a growing hunger — not for food but for company, for someone with whom he could share his life. He obtained permission to have a visitor and began seeing a woman who also was an inmate in the prison. Their meetings were in the visitor's room, where they spoke through the heavy steel grill screen. In time, the two fell in love and were married, yet they were never together except to meet on opposite sides of the steel grill in the visitor's room.

Approaching his fortieth birthday, the prisoner became aware of another growing hunger — the passion to escape! "Madness!" warned his cautionary inner-self. "Stay here where you are, for who knows what it's like out there in the larger world." Yet this powerful urge to break out of prison grew, and the prisoner actually was able to escape several times. Each time, however, he would voluntarily return and ask to be reimprisoned.

The prisoner read countless books on escape and the biographies of famous escapees. Yet, although he continually plotted and dreamed of escaping, he never really seriously thought he could free himself from his prison. He found consolation in repeating the words another prisoner had once scrawled in pencil on a prison wall, "The only way to get out of here is in a coffin."

In his book **Look Homeward Angel**, *Thomas Wolfe wrote, "Naked and alone we came into exile. In her dark womb we did not know our mother's face; from the prison of her flesh have we come into the unspeakable and incommunicable prison of this earth.... Which of us has not remained forever prison-pent?" Indeed, who among us is not in some way penned or shut up, caged like a canary or confined in a zoo like a chimp born in captivity?*

After his baptism Jesus announced to his fellow Nazareth townsfolk his mission as a liberator, "I have come to set the prisoners free!"[1] Why are so many of his disciples still prison-pent?

[1] See Luke 4: 18

The Torture Chamber

"Teacher," complained a disciple, "I am never happy or satisfied with anything. I feel like I live inside a torture chamber and seem plagued by bad things always happening to me. Is my unhappiness simply the curse of having to live on earth?"

"If you feel," replied the teacher, "that you're living in a torture chamber, you could move somewhere else! Yet, where you live can be a perfectly good place if you realize that the source of your unhappiness is not a curse. Rather, it's because someone is torturing you."

"Ah, of course," said the student, "you mean the devil! The great fiend Satan is torturing me day and night because I'm on the spiritual path. My lack of happiness is part of the price for seeking God instead of the pleasures of the flesh!"

"Hold on," answered the teacher. "Don't go off wildly into other realms when your torturer is close to home."

"Tell me, then," begged the student, "who my torturer is so I can escape from him or her."

"To find your torturer," replied the teacher, "you must first recognize the torture chamber in which you are being tormented." The student sat wrapped like a mummy in confusion. So the teacher mercifully continued, "You'll find it on the top of your shoulders. Climb the ladder of discipline and, with patience and gentle persistence, remodel your torture chamber."

The Lord Buddha said, "With our thoughts we make our world. Think evil thoughts and evil will follow you as surely as the cart follows the ox. Think good thoughts and goodness will follow you all the days of your life."[1]

It is not the events of daily life that cause unhappiness but how our mind judges those events and how we think about them. Buddha and Jesus were aware of the enormous power of thoughts and their mysterious magnetic power to attract either good or evil. Jesus taught, "Seek first — with all your thoughts and actions — the reign of God and everything you need will come to you."[2] When we orient our mind to that basic Gospel message, goodness and happiness become constant companions.

Thus, the teacher encouraged the student to climb step-by-step, thought-by-thought, to convert his torture chamber into a pleasure dome.

"By your freedom," says Jesus, "all will know you are my disciples."
—Fragment 2, Syah Scroll, 5: 7

[1] The *Dhammapada*, The Sayings of the Buddha
[2] See Matthew 6: 33, Luke 10: 27

Get
your
head
out
of
your
heart
and
you'll
feel
much
better.

Front Page Parable

Know Your Bible

The teacher read from the newspaper, "It says here that an unidentified man stabbed David Fleigelman, age forty, at the Sephardic Center synagogue in Brooklyn, New York. According to the police report, the two men had been arguing about which one knew more about the Torah."

"I don't understand, Teacher — what is the parable?"

"Why, that's for you to discover!" the teacher replied. "You can begin by pondering why Jesus never told his disciples to become experts of the written scriptures."

"To really be somebody in this world," says Jesus, "become a nobody."
—Fragment 2, Syah Scroll, 5: 9

The Traveling Salesman

The traveling salesman arrived on the afternoon train carrying two suitcases. On the side of one was painted *Business* and on the other *Pleasure*. He rented a room at Mrs. Murphy's Boarding House, and whenever he went out, everyone in town knew where he was headed. If he left Mrs. Murphy's house carrying the suitcase labeled *Business*, they knew he was on his way to work, even if he were going out to dinner. If he left carrying the suitcase marked *Pleasure*, he was out to have fun, even if he were going to work.

The traveling salesman was never seen without one or the other of his suitcases, yet no one knew what was inside them. When asked, he would only grin, place his index finger to his lips and wink.

Regardless of the secret contents of the suitcases, everyone found him charming both in business and socially. He was always perfectly at home in any situation. While swapping jokes and stories with the guys, if the phone would ring, *snap-click* and he was all business. *Snap-click* was the sound of the latch on his suitcase, which he opened and shut so quickly that you couldn't see what was taken out of it or put into it.

Whenever someone was draining his patience, talking endlessly about some trivial matter, s*nap-click* and instantly the traveling salesman's temperament would be transformed into Buddha-like serenity. Yet, although his face was serene, you could see his left leg bobbing up and down like an oil rig.

While enjoying himself with friends at a cocktail party, if someone would grab his elbow, pull him aside and begin to monopolize him, his face would be that of a trapped animal. But, then, *snap-click* and in the flick of a latch, he would be the gracious, charming diplomat, eager to listen to the person's tale. As quickly as you can snap your fingers, his suitcase would be opened and closed, and the only indication it had even been unlatched was the faint *snap-click*.

His success socially and in business was due to his ability to be comfortable with anyone and in any situation. Everyone in town loved his company, and his name was on every guest list. Yet, like any traveling salesmen, the day came when it was time to move on to the next town.

However, tragically, on his way to the train station, he was crossing Main Street carrying his two suitcases when a driverless runaway truck struck him down and killed him. The truck's impact sent his suitcases flying out of his hands, high into the air and crashing back down to the street. As they hit the street, both suitcases split apart, scattering their contents on and around the body of the dead traveling salesman. The townsfolk gathered at the accident site stood openmouthed, for he lay dead in the street surrounded by hundreds of different lifelike masks!

Paul of Tarsus said, "Although I am free in regard to all, I have made myself a slave to all so as to win over as many as possible.... I have become all things to all...."[1] Was Paul a hypocrite? If being two-faced is a vice, when can such a vice become a virtue? Moreover, what is necessary to convert a vice into a virtue?

[1] 1 Corinthians 9: 19, 22

The Sentence

They were sentenced to silence—period! There were those occasions, however, when they were given a brief parole for short periods of time and allowed to speak out loud — but only in chorus. Ironclad was the law that under no circumstance were they ever allowed to speak to one another. As a result, they spent most of their lives as silent as Trappist monks. Sadly, such was the fate of written words, who from the moment of their birth were ink-imprisoned in paper penitentiaries called books, bibles, reports, newspapers and letters.

Late one night, the Author fell asleep with pen in hand, tired from creative composition. The words she had written were birthed one-by-one with loving, imaginative, poetic care. She prided herself on her creativity, her ability to take ordinary letters of the alphabet and artfully arrange them in combinations of breathtaking freshness and homelike familiarity.

The Author slept soundly at her desktop, her head resting on her right arm under which lay a half-filled page. To the right of the page lay an old-fashioned quill pen whose point was still wet with ink. As the clock struck the magical hour of midnight, two words on the last sentence she had written broke the law and began to speak. "My father was Greek and my mother Latin," said the long word with great pride.

"Well, I'm pureblooded French," its neighbor replied in a musical voice while holding its head high.

The midnight magic began to spread down the sentence as other words began to speak. Although they spoke aloud, they didn't address each other. Rather, they simply identified themselves and their heritage. Within the sentence were immigrant words with Spanish, German, Anglo-Saxon and even Hebrew passports. Other words were hybrids with mixed blood, while some were slang or street words, who didn't know the identity of their fathers. While these latter words were not as yet recorded in the Big Blue Book, in time the descendants of these alien words would eventually come to be accepted.

The sentence also contained words so vulgar as to be judged obscene. They were shunned by the others, who called them "dirty words." The noble, poetic sounding words, whom fate and the Author had forced to share the same sentence with those of lesser birth, said to themselves, "The Author surely didn't write those words that way. They began as good words, but they perverted themselves. For does not each word penned have a free will?"

Some other words said aloud, "These dirty words have been cursed from birth. They are abominable in the eyes of God, a threat to the moral order. Unless they change, they should be banished or destroyed."

While in the midst of these tirades some words wished to take action against others, the words remained largely unrelated. For they basically spoke in soliloquies rather than in dialogue. Although some words in the sentence had college degrees and were used by great scholars, not even they knew the secret of the sentence. Since the words only spoke about themselves and never really spoke to one another, they did not know the meaning of the sentence in which they lived!

Not only Jesus, but each child of God is a word of God. If you knew the meaning of your life sentence, how do you think it would affect the way you relate to the other words in your sentence?

The Best Books

A seeker came to the teacher, asking, "I am interested in the spiritual quest—what books would you suggest I read?"

The teacher smiled and pointed to his empty bookshelves, saying, "The best books are people."

Wishing to justify himself, the seeker said, "Surely, a spiritual man like yourself would recommend that I read the Bible. Which translation of the Bible would you suggest?"

The teacher smiled faintly and replied, "The best translation of the Bible is a saint!"

"When you pray, don't be polite," says Jesus, "but pester God day and night."
—Fragment 2, Syah Scroll, 5: 13

The Doorknocker

One day in heaven as God was absorbed in a game of checkers with the old patriarch, Abraham, there came a loud knocking at heaven's front door. God shouted, "Will someone answer the door, please?" Turning back to the patriarch, God said, "It's your move, Abe." But as the unattended knocking grew louder, God yelled above the clamor, "Gabriel, would you please go and see who's at my door?"

Archangel Gabriel went to the doorway and opened a small peephole in the center of the door. After peering in every direction, Gabriel called back, "Lord God, I don't see anybody. Nobody's there!"

Ping, ping went Abraham's checker, capturing two of God's pieces. "Ah, yes, Lord God," said the old patriarch, "perhaps whoever was at your door was indeed a nobody, a person so small and insignificant as to be invisible! Or maybe it was some poor person begging for bread. Shouldn't you go and look for yourself?"

God stood up, the look of a double loser etched on the divine face, and went to the door. Opening the door, God found the porch empty. "Come and look for yourself, Abe. There's no one here."

"Ah, yes, Lord God, no doubt whoever *was* there grew tired of knocking and has now accepted being hungry or poor as part of your holy will. Don't holy scholars and theologians say that the purpose of prayer is to change us rather than trying to change you, O Absolute and Unchangeable One?"

Sitting down again at the checkerboard, God said, "Nonsense! Why come and knock at my door unless you are seeking something from me? Prayer is asking me for something and not just a means of accepting one's fate." Then, *ping, ping, ping,* God's checker captured three of Abraham's. As God's face beamed with a smile, there was a loud *rap, rap, rap* from the wall on God's left.

"Lord God," said Abraham, "now someone is knocking on the wall of your house, and knocking very loudly." Just then, Gabriel rushed over to the checkerboard table. "Lord God, excuse me, I'm sorry for interrupting your game, but the black hole in Galaxy MG-48X25 is clogged again!"

The pounding on the wall grew even louder as God first looked toward the wall, then down at the checkerboard and then up at Gabriel. "Send a plumber down to that galaxy," God said to the archangel, "and tell him this time to find out what the problem is! This is the third time this millennium that black hole has been clogged."

While God had turned to talk to Gabriel, Abraham had slyly enhanced his position by moving one of his checkers. "Ah, Lord God," he said, attempting to distract God, "I have a question for you. Blessed are you, for indeed your thoughts are not our thoughts, and especially your thoughts on prayer! Is it not true that any answer to a prayer has to be in harmony with your holy will, part of your holy plan?"

"What plan? You mean my dream?" asked God, suspiciously studying the revised position of the checkerboard after Abraham's move. God was about to move a checker when a loud *stomp, stomp, stomp* came from the ceiling. It sounded like someone violently stamping his or her feet on God's roof. The stomping grew louder until God shouted, "What do you want, for God's sake?"

"Father, please…" cried a soulful voice from the top of the chimney. "Ah," sighed God, placing a hand over the divine heart, "my child, quickly come down here to me! Abe, did you hear that? He called me, 'Father'!" God jumped up from the table and raced to the front door. Throwing open the door, God saw a needy man standing on the threshold. "Yes, my son, what is it you need?"

The timid man leaned over and whispered his petition in God's ear! "Ah, I understand your request," smiled God, "but why don't you try this on for size?" Then, to Abraham's surprise, God pointed an index finger at the man, and with a great s*wish* a blazing stream of scarlet-orange flames entirely engulfed the man! The hairs on his head stood on end, with their tips blazing like hundreds of Easter candles. Every cell of his body glowed like a neon lamp, until he was transformed into a blinding flash of lightning.

A split second later he was encompassed in a great mushroom cloud of white smoke. When the smoke cleared, all the flames had vanished. The man stood there, unscorched, wide-eyed, wearing a huge grin and looking ten years younger. He turned to God and said, "Thanks, God! Just what I needed!"

In Luke's Gospel, Jesus concluded his teaching on prayer with these words, "If you, with all your sins, know how to give your children good things, how much more will the heavenly Father give the Holy Spirit to those who ask him."[1]

Is not the best answer to any prayer the gift of God's Spirit? Reflect upon some present problem in your life, perhaps one that has been the subject of your prayers. How would you deal with your problem if you had the answered-prayer gift of the creative Holy Spirit?

[1] Luke: 11: 13

The Monster

For his secret scientific experiments the doctor had rented an old castle perched on a mountaintop near the northern Italian town of Frenzie. His wife and children had accompanied him to the castle, but he seldom spent any time with them, for day and night he was locked inside his laboratory. You see, the doctor was feverishly preoccupied in his experiment to create a new human being, one capable of functioning effectively in this complex world of high technology.

In the dead of night, the doctor would sneak out of his castle and visit local cemeteries to rob graves of spare body parts he needed to create his new-millennium human. His experiments were further complexified by the fact that he wanted to create a new double-sexed human being, who would be better able to adapt to modern life.

One night, as jagged bolts of lightning snaked down out of the belly of some dark storm clouds to illuminate his laboratory, the white-jacketed doctor labored at his operating table over a lifeless body he had successfully sewed together from various body parts. What his new-millennium man-woman now needed was not just a soul but the kind of energy that would enable the creature to act continuously. As thunder pounded on the roof of the castle, the doctor opened the skull of his lifeless creature and removed the human brain, which was now completely outdated for this ever-changing high-tech age. Then, in its place he inserted a computer-brain, which he had programmed to perform at twice the speed of light and with action-packed capabilities to handle back-to-back projects, tasks and commitments.

With this new brain, a great variety of human

activity — work, meals, entertainment, education, visiting friends — could all be accomplished almost instantly. Moreover, his new creature would never grow tired or need sleep. His new-millennium man-woman would know the ecstatic joy of perpetual motion and instant global communication.

The brain surgery completed, the doctor removed his surgical gloves and went to the wall covered with electrical panels containing all kinds of switches and round, glowing dials. Then he yanked down a large electrical circuit breaker. With a *zap-crackle-pop-swish* a searing beam of white exploded in sputtering electricity. It zigzagged down and surged into the lifeless monster on his operating table. When the smoke had cleared, the new-millennium woman-man slowly opened its large eyes and then leaped off the table.

She/he raced wildly around the laboratory, doing three or four things at the same time: ordering a fast food lunch, simultaneously answering calls on twin cell phones while sending three fax messages and writing an E-mail to a good friend. As the monster feverishly raced around in circles from task to task in the laboratory, the mad scientist of Frenzie triumphantly opened a bottle of vintage champagne to celebrate.

The monster's twin cell phones, pager and three faxes were all ringing at the same time, demanding instant attention, while its voice mail spoke in a Babel of a hundred voices all at once. In the midst of this mayhem, the monster's schedule-agenda machine's built-in emergency alarm began clanging loudly, "You're Late…You're Late…You're Late…."

The monster suddenly stopped and stood as still as a statue. Then, just as suddenly, like an overdue volcano, it erupted. It began screaming and hammering its computerized head with both fists. Again the monster came to a sudden stop, but this time it slowly turned toward its creator, Dr. Franticstein. To the doctor's horror, the monster came stomping toward him, roaring in great rage.

Dr. Franticstein madly ran from his laboratory, screaming at his family to leave the castle and flee the raging monster. From that day onward, the new-millennium monster, now known by the last name of his-her creator — Franticstein — pursued the poor doctor no matter where in the world he tried to escape.

Two millenniums ago the Roman philosopher Lucius Seneca wrote, "Everyone has time if he likes. Business runs after nobody; people cling to it of their own free will and think that to be busy is a proof of happiness." If in the hope of adapting yourself to the ever-increasing pace of a technological culture, you are redesigning yourself, ponder the fate of Dr. Franticstein. Beware of creating a monster that is subject to outbursts of raw irritability and rage. Be aware too that rushaholism creates listless lovers, forgetful friends, inattentive intimates, distracted devotees and pygmy attention spans.

Then, remember Jesus' parable about the rich man who built bigger barns to house his large harvest. God says to him, "Fool! This night your life shall be required of you, so where will all this piled up wealth go then?"[1] In light of our already very rich technology, is it not wiser to grow rich in the sight of God than to lose your soul by trying to grow richer still in the world's eyesight?

[1] Luke 12: 20

*Those who pray
on the run*

soon become Breathless.

Glory to God

"On Sundays at the time of the collection," said the student, "we are asked to give some of our money. Since we have money, we are able to give some of it away. At the beginning of the Liturgy," the student continued, "we also pray the ancient hymn *Glory to God in the Highest*. Teacher, tell us how is it possible to give glory to God if we don't have glory to give away?"

"In one sense," replied the teacher, "we need to give glory to God in the face of all our gifts and accomplishments. Indeed, because that's where the glory belongs, giving it to God is an act that grounds us in humility, in reality.

"On the other hand, you raise a very good question. You can't give away what you don't have!"

"I know how to acquire wealth so as to give it away," replied the student, "but how do I acquire the kind of glory to give to God which is not just words?"

The teacher smiled like the sun breaking through a heavily overcast sky. "St. Irenaeus, a bishop and martyr of the second century, said, 'The glory of God is a man or woman fully alive.' Glory is not given to God by great cathedrals or gorgeous stained glass windows, but rather by a person becoming fully alive! So, strive to be as fully alive as you can and know that, as you do, you are truly giving glory to God."

"Forget the future," says Jesus. "It's only today blown up like a balloon. So fill each day as full as possible."

—Fragment 2, Syah Scroll, 5: 21

The Mirror Miracle

"Bless me, Father, for I have sinned," John whispered through the aged wooden confessional grill, "but I also want to be holy."

From behind the curtain of the screen the voice replied, "Hmm, interesting," in response to the confession. "Yes, yes, my son. Now, for your penance say one Our Father and one Hail Mary and go in peace."

"Father, I do not want to go in peace," John said. "I am restless until I can begin to become holy. Will you help me? I have been told you are holy, so you must know the secret. Please, share it with me."

In the darkness, he could hear the priest sucking his tongue as if it were rummaging around in the moist cave of his mouth for the right words. "You were misinformed," the old priest said through the grill, "I am not holy. Only God is holy. Now, go in peace, and try to sin no more."

"Father," John pleaded, "are you telling me that the secret to holiness is to be virtuous and sin no more?"

"No, my son," the priest answered, "that is not the secret, but it does help."

Leaning closer to the grill, John begged, "What else must I do to be holy? Please, give me some clue!"

A cough and throat clearing preceded the message from the other side. "Others are waiting, my son, waiting to confess their sins. The confessional is a place to take secret things away, not to give them out. Now, go in peace."

His fingers gripping the confessional grill, John answered, "I will be glad to go, Father, but only after you've told me the secret."

"Communion with God is the gift given to the virtuous," the priest said with a great sigh, "but it is an incomplete communion and so comes short of true holiness. To be holy is to…to be Godlike, for God alone is holy."

Pressing his face as close as possible to the wooden, sin-stained grill through which so many dark secrets had passed, John said, "Yes, yes, Father, but how, then, do I become like God?"

"Ah, my son, you must return to the beginning. Yes, yes, it is there in the garden that you'll find the secret, for in the beginning were not humans made in the image of God? Alas, now that image is turned upside down. Go home and look in the mirror. Now, go in peace." Then the old priest slammed shut the sliding grill door of the confessional.

"He just wanted to get rid of me," John said to himself as he left the church, "with that stuff about going home and looking in a mirror." He drove home, his heart filled with disappointment. Three days later, awakening from a restless night's sleep, he recalled the old priest's words, "…now that image is turned upside down."

He immediately went into the bathroom and tried to turn his head so he could see his image upside down, but all he saw was a contorted face. Then going to a full-length mirror, he stood on his head and looked at his image. He screamed aloud — not from the blood rushing to his brain, but in delight. "Thank God, the old priest did share with me the secret of holiness!"

Now, John lived in a small town where everyone knew everyone else, so soon all the townsfolk were talking about the "new" John. While he continued to practice his faith, going to church each Sunday, he also daily practiced something else. John was now constantly checking his image in every mirror, store window and shiny surface he passed.

The parade of years marked by fidelity to his daily discipline bore fruit in two strange ways. John became known for his vanity, as he was always looking at his reflection. But he was also known as the happiest and most contented man in town.

To be sure, no one ever called him holy, since he was not known to be particularly pious or saintly. Instead, he was known for his smile! Everyone agreed that it left a lasting impression. Some even called it "John's autograph."

The book of Genesis states that God made humans in the divine image. And Aristotle, the ancient Greek fountain of knowledge, added that, of all living creatures, humans are the only ones endowed with the ability to laugh.

A smile is the outward sign of a laughing soul. And the wrinkled brow of a frown viewed upside down looks like the lines made by a smile. Mindful that your face reflects the face of your soul, examine yourself frequently in the mirror to see if your birthright as God's image is right-side up.

The Fish

"Father, give me some bread, for I am hungry," begged the son.

"Son, this is better than bread," the father said as he handed his son a dead fish. "Trust me, I know what's best for you, for I am your father and I love you."

The hungry boy looked at his fish, which had been dead for some time. While he didn't understand, he trusted his father. The next day, the boy went to his mother and implored, "Mother, please give me some bread, for I am hungry."

His mother looked at him, then at the dead fish in his hand and, smiling, said, "Son, men do not live on bread alone."

The boy was very hungry, yet the long-dead fish didn't look appetizing in any way. So to still the rat of hunger nibbling away in his belly, he tried feeding it with treats from sidewalk vendors: ice cream, hot tamales and cappuccino lattés. But the beast of hunger only grew larger.

Meanwhile, the fish the boy had been given grew deader by the day. Like all dead things, it began to stink. When he complained about this to his mother, she told him, "Burn some incense; it will mask the odor of the dead fish."

Years passed, and the boy grew into a man. He married and himself had a son. One day, his son came and begged him for bread. "Here, my son," said the father. "Trust me, I know what's best for you. I am your father and I love you." And he handed his son a petrified fish.

The hungry boy stroked the fish's chilly, stony scales and licked his fingers just as he had seen his father and mother and grandparents do. "Finger-licking good," he said aloud with a weak, skinny smile, echoing what he had heard his parents and grandparents say.

This boy himself grew into a man and married, and he also had a son. His son came and begged, "Father, I am hungry, give me some bread." The father smiled, for he knew what to do. "Here, my son," he said, "this is what my father gave to me and his father's fathers handed on to their sons. Trust me, son, for I love you." And he handed his son the now ancient, dead petrified fish.

The son graciously thanked his father, and not wishing to offend him, took the long-dead fish. But then, going out into the backyard, the boy buried the petrified fish in an unmarked grave.

Many traditions that have been handed on from generation to generation are rightly treasured as nourishing lifelines that express a sacred history. Not all traditions, however, remain life-giving. In the Book of Revelation, rephrasing Isaiah, Jesus describes in a sentence the ministry of Christ, the Messiah: "Behold I make all things new!" In the days when those words were written, the fish was a secret code sign for a follower of Jesus the Galilean. Which of the fish that remain today as expressions of the Christian symbol are fresh and which are petrified?

The Worst of All Sins

The Sacred Congregation for the Holy Inquisition of Heretical Error was its official name, but it was simply known as the Inquisition, a name that caused hearts to tremble. The Inquisition was composed of overly zealous clerics who labored day and night to uncover dangerous heretics promoting novel ideas contrary to Faith and Holy Scripture. Those found guilty were excommunicated and punished with the zeal of doctors removing a cancerous growth.

Deep within the Inquisition's medieval head-quarters, a secret court of clerical judges had debated for days over which sin was the most dangerous to the soul. They needed to determine the most mortal of sins with some immediacy since the pope was to announce this decision in a new encyclical. On the seventh day a skinny cloud of black smoke curled up from the chimney of their chambers, signaling that they had reached a decision.

The pope's encyclical letter naming the most evil of all sins was read aloud from the steps of every cathedral. The gathered crowds shuddered as it was sternly announced, "All found guilty of practicing this most mortal sin will be excommunicated, and their foreheads branded with a large letter *A*." The secret agents of the Inquisition at once began to round up those suspected of this gravest of all sins.

Fear gripped the hearts of the wealthy and the poor, those in cities and the country, and, surprisingly, even those in monasteries and convents. Terror swept the land as the Inquisition began constructing wooden judgment stands in every village square. On these platforms blazed fires in which were placed branding irons bearing a large letter *A*.

Doomsday arrived, and crowds of suspected

sinners were herded to the judgment stands. The black-hooded officers of the Inquisition were deaf to the pleas of the condemned for mercy. "No mercy will be yours! For the Lord himself has strictly warned you to avoid this sin," cried the Inquisitioners over the screams of the guilty being marked by the sizzling branding iron.

*Did the letter **A** stand for Adultery, Atheism, Abortion, Alcoholism, Abolition or any rebellion against the Authority of the Church?*

Perhaps it stands for Avarice! While sexual urges decline with age, this is a sin that only grows stronger with age." A penny saved is a penny earned" is the beatitude of the thrifty. Yet, when does being thrifty graduate into vicious greed? When does the virtue of being careful with your money become the vice of being tight with your love, talents and time? In this light, Jesus teaches, "Beware of avarice, greed, in all its many forms."[1]

The best-known antidote for creeping greed is generosity run amuck, being drunkenly generous — in the image of the Giver of All Gifts — at all times and in all things.

[1] Luke 12: 15

Front Page Parable

Holy or Unholy Madness?

"Here's an interesting article from Eugene, Oregon," said the teacher as he read from the front page of the newspaper. "It tells about a former marine who's the leader of a new religious cult preparing for the approaching end of the world.

"The cult is called the Brotherhood, and the followers, having renounced all ties to society, are grouped into eight to ten nomadic units or cells. They must abstain from all sex and must spend their time in pairs. The members of the Brotherhood wear only sandals and simple homemade tunics, even in the winter. They believe that money is dirty and avoid handling it. Their only food is garbage, which the members collect by rummaging through supermarket dumpsters."

"Garbage!" gagged the student. "They really sound weird."

"It says here," the teacher continued, "that they are very careful to remove all traces of rot, since the Brotherhood is strict about being physically clean in preparation to meet their maker."

"It still sounds weird," replied the student." Who in their right mind would join such a cult?"

"While their poverty was based on solidarity with the poor, I'll bet St. Francis of Assisi and St. Clare of Assisi would join a group like the Brotherhood if they were here today," said the teacher. "This is the sort of radical poverty that they embodied and wanted their followers to embrace. Rome and the hierarchy wouldn't let them live out such an all-encompassing poverty, so they compromised their dream to stay inside the fold. Yet Francis surely must have been saddened by that compromise. Poverty is a sign, and in every age the world is only awakened by signs of radical poverty like eating only from garbage dumpsters! Would church authorities today affirm or even allow any recognized religious group to live such an unbounded poverty?"

"Teacher," asked the student, "surely that cult group in Eugene, Oregon, is a bunch of loonies. Their lifestyle is madness, isn't it?"

"Madness," answered the teacher ever so softly. "Yes, madness is the sign of those who are mentally disoriented — and also of those who are mystically reoriented."

Soul-Dead

The Teacher required all new students to take a complete medical examination, which he himself gave them. Taking the pulse of his newest applicant for spiritual training, he shook his head sadly, saying, "Soul-dead." His hand still on the shocked student's wrist, he continued, "Good, your heart's still beating, and you're still breathing, so there's hope."

"Teacher," replied the shocked applicant, "how can I be soul-dead and still be alive? Isn't the soul immortal — as Plato said — the very principle of life itself?"

"Yes and no," replied the teacher placing his ear to an odd-looking medical instrument, which he held against the applicant's chest. "Please refrain from speculations about Greek philosophy for the moment. Be quiet, now, and breathe deeply. I'm taking the temperature of your heart.

"Just as I suspected," the teacher said, raising his head from the applicant's chest. "It's neither hot nor cold. I regret to inform you that you are afflicted with *Susto*." Large question marks filled both of the applicant's eyes. The teacher continued, "Translation: You've lost your soul! As I said, you're soul-dead." Standing and pointing to the door, he concluded, "I'm afraid you've failed the examination. I'm sorry, but without a soul it would be a waste of your time and mine for you to become a student of the spiritual path."

"Surely, Teacher," begged the applicant, "there must be some cure — a medical procedure…."

His hand on the doorknob, the teacher nodded, "Yes, but I fear you'll find the cure too painful and too long." Then he gestured toward the open doorway.

But the applicant begged, "Teacher, I'll do anything. With all my heart I long to find the Way. Tell me, what is the cure?"

"Good, your desire for a cure is encouraging, for it's a terrible thing to be afflicted with *Susto*," the teacher said. "While there are various remedies, the quickest way to recover one's lost soul is to do the following: Leave the city at once and go to the nearest forest or wilderness area you can find. Camp out there without a tent, sleeping bag, port-a-potty, clock, radio or other such modern comforts. Stay there day and night until the trees, wild grasses, birds, wild creatures and even the bugs begin to talk to you."

As the applicant looked in total disbelief, the teacher added, "Sorry, I told you the cure was painful. There are slower means, but I don't recommend them."

Cultures with roots deep in Greek philosophy usually maintain that the soul is immortal, yet other cultures believe the soul can be stolen and can even die.

Susto *is a contemporary Hispanic term for the loss of soul.* ***Susto*** *is often seen in tribal peoples who are suddenly urbanized, as now frequently happens in third world countries. Yet soul loss is so common a condition in the Western world, which is radically divorced from nature, that it is usually not even acknowledged.*

A good daily exercise for ***Sustoites*** *would be to stare at something in creation until it begins to stare back. As Gerard Manley Hopkins said, "What you look at hard seems to look at you." These wise words could be rephrased, "What you look at intensely awakens you to the reality that everything is alive." All creation looks at and can talk to those who are not soul-dead.*

The Secret Skill

"Teacher, I believe you know all things. Teach me the secret of how to be happy," begged the student.

"All right, but where would you like to begin?" smiled the teacher.

"Show me how to control the weather so that every day may be bright and sunny, for I feel sad when we have cloudy or bad weather, and I have a hard time adjusting to extreme temperatures."

"You can limit yourself to air-conditioned, climate controlled environments," said the teacher, "or you could go in search of a place where the sun shines every day of the year!" As the student pondered departing on such a search, the teacher added, "However, the weather is ultimately beyond human control, and one can be equally unhappy on a sunny day as on a cloudy one."

Musing for a moment on this answer, the student replied, "Teacher, you are wise and correct. Show me, then, how to control the financial markets, stocks and bonds. If I become a millionaire, then I can be happy."

The teacher responded, "You can invest a good deal of time and energy becoming astute in financial planning and recognizing trends in the market." Then he sat in silence until the student had time to think about the implications of this question and response.

"I'm not sure," the student finally said, "the investment is worth it. I know that wealth is not the source of happiness either, since there are so many un-happy millionaires." The teacher nodded in agreement.

"Could you, then, share with me," continued the student, "the knowledge of how to control my arms and legs. If I were gracefully coordinated, I could become a great athlete or ballet dancer. I could be famous — a star with thousands of fans. Then I would be happy."

"It is indeed a blessing to be graceful, on whatever

level. But if that is what you desire, you don't need me," the teacher replied. "What you need is a coach! Moreover, are there not as many unhappy famous people as rich people?"

After a long, empty silence the student again spoke, "Teacher, I see where this is leading. Is the secret that it is not possible for us who live in this valley of tears to find lasting happiness?"

"No, on the contrary, it is possible. For happy are those who are in control," the teacher replied with a smile. The student looked completely confused, but the teacher said, "Put on your thinking cap. Then you'll know the only thing in this world you can control."

Among the paradoxes of life is that the only thing we can control is what we seldom if ever even attempt to control — those thoughts we wish to entertain. Those who put on their thinking cap and make it their hard hat, their working cap, find the secret of happiness.

The path of daily life is scattered with land mines: problems, disappointments, afflictions and failures — all of which cause suffering. Yet, these are not the sources of unhappiness. That, rather, is determined by how we judge and think about our difficulties. We can, to our great benefit, learn to control our thought patterns — we can learn to align our mind to the mind of Christ.

The control of an untrained adult mind is as challenging as controlling a spoiled child's behavior. It requires more rigid discipline than toilet training. It demands constant vigilance wedded to patience. Yet, practicing with gentleness and firmness, we can understand the enlightening words of the Lord Buddha, "With our thoughts we make our world."[1]

[1] The *Dhammapada*, The Sayings of the Buddha

Have a Good Day

One day, the teacher and a student were walking on the road when a man came rushing out of the bushes directly toward them. The teacher stopped and, reaching into his pocket, said, "Hello, stranger. Today's your lucky day! I'd like to gift you with my wallet and my watch!"

The man was stunned at this response, but he snatched the teacher's wallet and watch and then ran away into the woods. The teacher called after him, "Friend, no need to run. Those were gifts. Have a good day, for I certainly am!"

Even more stunned was the student, who asked, "Teacher, why did you give that man your wallet and watch, and why did he run away without even saying thank you? Was he a robber?"

"He would have been," the teacher chuckled with great delight. "Remember, it's always better to give something away before it's taken away from you."

One moment life is like Santa Claus, and the next it's like Jessie James! Life both gives gifts and robs us of those gifts. Aging and Time hide and lie in wait for us along the highway of life, threatening to steal any of the abundant gifts that are ours, whether wealth or good health, hearing or sight, ease of physical movement or even the greatest of all gifts, life itself. Happy are those who, with great delight, give life's gifts away freely instead of having them taken away in a violent struggle.

Front Page Parable

Spiritual Face-Lift

"Ah, listen to this parable," said the teacher, looking up from his newspaper. "Here's an article titled, *Spiritual Cosmetics*. The article quotes the *New York Times* about today's new booming market in holy cosmetics. It says these spiritually enriched bubble baths, lipstick and special night creams are purported to give consumers greater confidence and knowledge of their higher selves." The teacher lowered the newspaper and smiled.

"Weird," said the student, "but what's the parable?"

"Put on a holy face!" replied the teacher. "Only, spiritual cosmetics are not new; putting on a spiritual face is an ancient custom. Surface spirituality has been practiced in all times and all religious cultures. Indeed, it's easier, faster and more comfortable to become holy by a refreshing bubble bath than to be bathed in fire."

"Fire?" stammered the startled student.

"As old John the bath-giver said," the teacher concluded, "'when he comes, he will baptize you in the Holy Spirit and *fire.*'"[1]

[1] Matthew 3: 11

The Miracle

The Smiths built their own house, but they had a lot of help from their parents, family and friends. Though it was more than livable, the Smith House was not a very happy house. Because the hands that had built it were many and often passionless, the house had little cohesion.

One late afternoon, about an hour before sunset, a tornado came roaring like a freight train out of the sky toward their house. Mr. Smith wildly pushed his wife and children into the basement and fell to his knees, praying for a miracle. Within seconds, the deadly sky train from hell roared directly over their house, leveling it to its basement foundation.

When the family emerged safely from the cellar, all that was left of their house was a pile of twisted timbers. They huddled close together and stood gaping at their personal disaster when the sun broke through the dark clouds. It cast long yellow rays of light on the ugly hill of twisted lumber and fragments of broken furniture. A single sunbeam glistened off a hammer that had been dropped there by the tornado.

"It's a miracle," Mrs. Smith wept, "that all of us were spared. Thank God. Oh, thank God!"

Her husband nodded, but he thought to himself, "Yes, but the miracle I prayed for was that my house would also be spared. Now what will we do?" Looking around, he saw the homes of their friends and neighbors were also destroyed. Their neighborhood was as a disaster zone, and he realized he could expect no help from them to rebuild his home.

Mr. Smith walked over to the pile of wreckage left by the tornado and picked up the hammer. "It's not mine, and there's no name on it. Who knows where this thing came from?"

The next morning he began the work of pulling nails out of boards with that hammer. The whole family began stacking the good boards one-by-one in a pile. Husband, wife and children worked side-by-side as together they began to rebuild their house, this time without any help from others. As their house slowly rose up, it seemed the husband grew taller, the wife more loving and the children in mutual respect. The rebuilt Smith house was finally completed. Yet the family about to move into it was far different from the family that had lived in the previous house.

On the day they moved into their rebuilt house, the first thing Mr. Smith did was to place a gold-framed glass box over the fireplace. In the box was the hammer left by the tornado, the hammer with which they had rebuilt their home. The Smiths called the gold-framed box "the Shrine of the Miracle."

Which house was miraculously saved: the physical house or the Smith's family structure? Is their rebuilt house an example of the old adage: "If you don't have a wolf howling at your front door, then hire one"?

The Jewish Talmud records the rabbis as saying, "Don't rely on a miracle." The Jewish mystics also say, "The world cannot exist without miracles." Are you today helping to rebuild the world by "working on" a miracle?

The Atheist

The professor was intelligent and knowledgeable, even if he really wasn't a professor. His friends had given him that nickname because he was always discussing philosophical subjects and questioning every belief.

As a child he had been a believer, and as a teenager few doubts ever visited his heart. However, as an adult serious questions began to sleep overnight in his mind. Because these visiting doubts departed each morning at sunrise, the professor liked to joke that he was a night-duty agnostic.

He delighted in discussing his numerous doubts over a glass of beer with his buddies at the neighborhood bar and grill. Whenever his friends would raise an objection to one of his new agnostic considerations, the professor always answered, "Yes, I agree. But who knows for sure? I mean, who can *really* prove it's true beyond any doubt?"

Then, one evening, he boldly announced to his friends at the neighborhood bar, "I am no longer an agnostic; I'm an atheist! About this, I no longer doubt; I simply do not believe!" Then he shared with them the belief he had abandoned.

To this bold declaration of disbelief, his friends replied, "Professor, are you hiding something from us? You don't have some incurable disease, do you?"

Ordering another cup of strong black coffee, he shook his head, "No, I'm as healthy as any of you. I simply do not believe in *that* any longer. I am an atheist."

Astonished, they asked, "But all the evidence, professor — except for rare exceptions — how can you deny it?"

Holding up his hand, he proclaimed, "Friends, the discussion is ended! Now, it's time to go — but not home. I'm going for a walk, a very long walk."

Concerned about his emotional stability, his friends insisted on accompanying him. So, he began his long walk, stopping only to drink cup after cup of strong black coffee.

For three days and three nights he walked, his friends taking turns to walk with him. By nightfall of the third day he was so exhausted that he began to stumble and stagger. Yet he resisted his friend's efforts to make him sit and rest. Instead, he forced himself to keep walking, fearful that if he ever stopped and sat he would fall asleep. For, you see, his fear was tied in to his particular brand of atheism: He no longer believed that if he went to sleep he would awaken again the next morning!

As the moon rose that third night, the exhausted atheist stumbled for the last time before finally collapsing to the ground. As he fitfully fell fast asleep, the friend who was with him at the time gently covered him with a blanket and kept vigil at his side until morning.

Sleep is a sacrament. It's God's Good Night News. The fear of the dark — whether it afflicts small children or even adults — is linked to fears, especially the fear of death. However, 365 times a year, the fear of not waking up again is disproved. By the age of fifty, not counting naps, you have awakened from sleep over 18,250 times! So, why question your awakening after your final sleep of death when you've already experienced so many personal resurrections? If you need any more assurance, consider the Good News Great Awakening of the carpenter of Nazareth.

Distractions in Prayer

"Teacher," begged the student, "whenever I pray, I am constantly bothered by distractions. Please tell me how to get rid of them."

"Don't!" smiled the teacher.

"Don't?" asked the startled student. "Are you saying I shouldn't try to remove them from my prayer?"

"First of all, your mind is always crowded with thoughts," replied the teacher. "You only become aware of that fact when you try to pray. Instead of trying to remove them, each distraction in prayer can become a step or rung on a ladder, helping you ascend or descend to a new level of devotion in your prayer."

"But, Teacher," the student gasped, "sometimes in my prayer I am distracted by sexual fantasies. Surely, they are from the devil and must be banished!"

"Is not everything," the teacher answered quietly, "created by God? Even your sexual thoughts find their source in the All Holy One who created all that exists in heaven and on earth. While any thought can lead you into sin, if you use it as a prayer can it not just as well lead you back to God?"

The two sat in silence for awhile, until the teacher said, "Go now and climb the ladder of your prayer, one distraction after another, until you find your home in God."

Distractions in prayer are commonly the second greatest problem of those striving to pray, the first being actually finding time to pray. Prayer can become a battlefield on which we constantly war against distractions, only to become frustrated at losing most, if not all, our battles. Over the centuries, spiritual masters have suggested various ways to deal with distractions. Some have advised banishing them. Others have counseled treating them like flies and ignoring them or using them as reminders that we haven't yet gone deeply enough into our prayer.

In this parable, the teacher's response to distractions is based on a teaching by the Jewish mystic Ba'al Shem Tov, who taught this revolutionary way to deal with distractions. If God is ever present, then why not use every distraction as a holy rung on the ladder of prayer?

"Be stopped by no obstacle," says Jesus, "go over, under or through it."
—Fragment 2, Syah Scroll, 5: 17

Rosarita's Second Childhood

Little Rosarita was a superb natural acrobat. She was as much at home walking across the high wire at the top of the circus tent as any child walking across a playground. Her father, mother and two brothers were all acrobats, the Amazing Flying Sambinis, who had entertained circus crowds for years. While renowned for their aerialist skills, none of them had the grace and fearless agility of little Rosarita, who never used a net. Without a trace of fear she would let go of her father's strong wrists and, flipping head over heels, would fly across the vast empty space at the top of the tent before landing in one of her brothers' waiting arms. Rosarita was uncalculating — totally free and spontaneous in her somersaults on the high wire. Her mother, however, worried about her and continuously cautioned her, "Rosarita, be careful!"

Her father guarded his Little Rosarita like a precious crown jewel, not because she was the star of their family circus act, but because she was so wonderfully innocent. He was aware that her fearless grace came because she was still untouched by harm in any way.

The day came, however, as everyone knew it would, when Little Rosarita lost her innocence and fell from the high wire. Now, she knew fear in all its variety of flavors. She began to plan how she would answer a question and to practice standing so that the light would reflect best off her face. Little Rosarita now had a new act. She was known as Revolving Rosarita and became famous for her ability to hang by one hand from the high wire and whirl endlessly around and around. Yet, no longer did she fly effortlessly from her father's arms into the arms of her brothers. And now she always used a net! Maturity has its price.

Yet, despite her success, Rosarita ached to fly again. She began to practice trying not to think ahead about how she should act or what she should say or not say. She would dangerously disregarded how she might appear if she cried or giggled in public. Daily she practiced the art of not rehearsing her behavior in life. It took great discipline and training for her to begin to act spontaneously again, but Rosarita was determined to fly.

Once more, her mother began to worry because for a second time Rosarita was becoming too natural. To her mother, adults who become innocent, who again become childlike, are either fools or saints. And she knew that both of these are dangerous.

"Father, today I'm ready to fly again," Rosarita finally told her father, "and without a net!" In vain her mother pleaded with her, and her worried father said, "My dear one, my wrists are not as strong as they were years ago. I fear…."

Her brothers were also anxious and said, "Rosarita, we also are no longer as young and strong as we once were. We worry that…."

She only smiled and said, "Tomorrow, I fly again."

The next day Rosarita flew from her father's arms gracefully across the top of the tent into her brothers' arms as everyone far below in the circus audience gasped aloud in wonder. "However does she do that?" a clown asked the ringmaster.

Raising his hat high in a salute to the free-flying aerialist, the ringmaster replied, "You have to be graceful."

Perhaps our greatest achievement is to attain our second childhood. Often this is the negative term for seniors who become silly in their old age and again begin to act like little children. Yet true second childhood does not come naturally. It's an adult development gained only by great discipline. It is the grand paradox: One must consciously discipline oneself to become unconsciously undisciplined, to become spontaneously graceful.

True second innocence is not ignorant of the darkness of sin. And it is only by the grace of God that the fortunate ones somersault out of that dark self-consciousness, sin-consciousness and guilt back into the unrehearsed, fearless and graceful "glorious freedom of the children of God."[1] Blessed are those who try to live there. Blessed are those who at any age go to the College of Unlearning to learn how to be liberated, who learn how to fly without a net.

[1] Romans 8: 21

The Spirit-filled keep no rules and follow no maps or charts 'cause they're

Blowin' in the Wind.

The Pearly Gates

One day Jesus opened the Pearly Gates and carefully looked around outside. No one was waiting in line to enter, so he stepped outside and hung a sign on the gates of heaven. Printed in bold letters was the message: *No Deaf, Blind or Physically Handicapped Allowed!* With a loud clang, a smiling Jesus slammed shut the massive gates that were decorated with thousands of glistening pearls.

As expected, there soon gathered outside the gates of heaven an angry crowd of deaf, blind and physically handicapped, along with members of the American Civil Liberties Union. Others joined them to demonstrate against that ugly sign on heaven's gate. Some of those in the crowd carried placards saying, *Discrimination Is Sinful* or *Heaven Has Unfair Admission Policies* or *Jesus Discriminates!* or even *A Heaven Not Open to the Handicapped Should Go to Hell!*

The blind rhythmically pounded their white canes against heaven's gates in cadence with others' angrily shouted slogans, but no one appeared from inside heaven to respond. Then, around sunset, Jesus opened the tall pearly gates and peered out at the angry mob. As he did, a hush fell over the crowd. Looking intently at the crowd of angry demonstrators, Jesus said, "The only thing I have to say to you is what Pontius Pilate said, 'What I have written, I have written!'"[1] Then Jesus slammed shut the gates of heaven.

When the crowds asked Jesus the number of those who would be saved, he replied that it would be a surprise! Jesus spoke of pious people who came to the gates of heaven begging entrance, saying, "We ate and drank with you and listened to you teach in our streets." But Jesus replied, "I do not know you. Away with you!"[2] The same Jesus had also said, "Let those with eyes see and those with ears hear — and then put into practice what they see and hear. Repent and believe in the Good News."[3]

Even more forcefully, Jesus added, "Unless you repent, you will all perish."[4] Those blind and deaf to his good news become his physically disabled disciples because they fail to put into practice what they hear — and so find the gates of heaven shut to them. What is the full meaning of "to repent and believe the Good News?"

Once people feared dying in the state of sin. Fear, more, dying in your same old unrepentant state.

"If you're not living on the edge," says Jesus, "you're not living in me."
—Fragment 2, Syah Scroll, 5: 16

---

[1] John 19: 22
[2] See Luke 13: 22-30
[3] See Mark 1: 15; Matthew 13: 10-13
[4] See Luke 13: 5

A Companion for Adam

Shortly after creating Adam, God began to worry about him because God could tell he wasn't happy. Knowing the source of his sadness, God said, "It's not good for man to be alone."

"Perhaps," said God, "I should create ten or twelve more Adams who could be his companions. "Yes, friends!" God said aloud with delight to all the heavenly host. "That's what my poor lonely Adam needs. These friends could divide into teams and play sports, or they could go hunting and camping together."

God went to the drawing board and quickly designed the new companions for Adam. But none of these beautiful designs ever left the drawing board. The Creator delayed, aware that for a time you have to live with whatever you create. Then God pondered aloud, "If I have one problem with my first man, will I not likely have ten new problems if I create ten more Adams?" So days in Eden passed, and Adam's sadness grew.

"Aha!" God exclaimed, awakening one morning with a new idea. "That's it! Rather than creating new creatures, I'll work a small miracle and simply redesign an existing one!" So, God worked the small miracle, then summoned Adam, saying, "I have solved the problem of your loneliness. Behold, Adam, your friend: dog!"

Dog became Adam's best friend; the two were constant companions. God smiled, knowing Adam was no longer lonely — at least for the present.

Fish Gotta Swim

"Teacher," asked the student, "why is it so difficult to love God?"

"Difficult?" replied the teacher. Then, after a moment he added, "I feel a song coming on," and he began singing,

> *Fish gotta swim, birds gotta fly,*
> *I gotta love my God till I die,*
> *Can't help loving that God of mine.*

"Shouldn't that correctly be sung, 'I gotta love one man till I die?'" asked the student. "You've got that old *Show Boat* melody, but…"

"Picky, picky," replied the teacher. "Granted, I made one slight change, but let those with ears hear."

"Hear what?" the student shot back.

"Just as birds naturally sing and fish swim, so to love God is only doing what comes naturally. It's not as difficult as you think; you just can't help loving God," the teacher said, still humming the melody of that Jerome Kern-Oscar Hammerstein song.

"What do you mean?" asked the student. "I have to consciously try to love God since that kind of love is supernatural, not natural."

"*Fish gotta swim, birds gotta fly, it ain't hard loving God till I die,*" sang the teacher as the student put his hands over his ears. "Your problem," said the teacher, "is your definition of God is catechism-narrow. I ask you, do you love life? Do you love to love and be loved?"

"Yes, but it's natural to love life and want more of it," answered the student, "and the same is true with love."

The teacher only smiled and walked away, still humming that haunting *Show Boat* tune.

The Secret of Fatima

"Teacher," began a student, "I have a question about the vision of Fatima, where Mary the Blessed Mother is said to have appeared in 1917 to three children, telling them to pray. When she first appeared to them, Jacinta was only six years old, Francisco seven and Lucy nine. I read a pamphlet which said that several days after their vision the three children were playing in the shade near the well. It was noon on a hot summer day when an angel appeared to them and said, 'Why are you playing? You must pray more.'"

"Yes," replied the teacher, "what is your question?"

"The priest who wrote the pamphlet said that the angel went on to declare that the capital sin of sloth isn't just ordinary laziness, but is laziness in spiritual matters. Teacher, what do you think about what the angel told the children? Should we pray more than we play?"

"What's the difference?" answered the teacher. "As long as you do either of them with all your heart. Pray and play — when you do one well, you are also doing the other!"

The best prayer — like the most creative work — always contains an element of play. Those who pray well, in the words of the wisdom of China, "...do it in the spirit of play. In this they are like children and in harmony with the Tao (the Way or Spirit)."[1]

[1] *Tao Te Ching*, Chapter 68

20/20 Vision

"Teacher," a student complained, "one of my brother students, whose name I won't mention, is a bad example to all of us. He loves to gossip about other students and point out their failings. And he even criticizes you! He's frequently absent from communal prayer and sleeps during meditation. I also hear that at night he sneaks out to visit the 'bad' girls in the village. Teacher, am I bound to challenge him face-to-face about these sins and failings? Tell me, what should I do?"

"Rather," said the teacher, "go to the village and get yourself a pair of glasses."

Blindness is perhaps the most common affliction, so both Jesus and Buddha tried to heal their disciples of it. At the heart of his teaching, the Lord Buddha said, "How easy it is to see your brother's faults, how hard to face your own."[1]

Likewise, the Lord Jesus said that those who see small sin splinters needing to be removed in the eyes of others really need 20/20 vision to help them remove the plank from their own eyes.[2]

[1] *Dhammapada*, Chapter 18
[2] See Luke 6: 41-42

Front Page Parable

Seeing the Inside on the Outside

"Ah, a curious historical note," said the teacher, reading from the newspaper's science section. "It's entitled 'Canals on Mars.'"

"That sounds interesting," said the student, "especially since they're planning a manned mission — or perhaps manned-womaned — mission to that planet."

"Indeed!" the teacher said. "The article relates that in 1906, at the beginning of the last century, the famed astronomer Percival Lowell announced from his observatory in Flagstaff, Arizona, that he had discovered canals on Mars. He detailed his discovery in his book *Mars as the Abode of Life,* saying the canals on Mars were red. He even charted them on detailed maps. Some schools went so far as to include Lowell's maps with the canals of the planet Mars in their atlases."

"But, teacher…" objected the student.

"Yes, I know," replied the teacher. "Today we know that there are no canals on Mars. Yet Lowell was so great an astronomer in those days that no one dared to contradict him. The very year before his Mars 'discovery,' Lowell proved the existence of another, unknown planet — which was confirmed in 1930, when the planet was given the name Pluto."

The teacher continued, "The article goes on to state that the famed astronomer suffered from a rare eye disease now known as Lowell's Syndrome. Under certain circumstances," the teacher interjected, "like looking through a telescope, it is possible for those so afflicted to see the veins in their own eyes!"

"And the parable in this, teacher?" replied the student.

"Consider what we might call 'casual eye syndrome' as the source of discrimination," said the teacher. "Those who see others as inferior because of their skin color, sexual orientation or religion — to mention only a few ways we discriminate — are they not like what Lowell saw on Mars? Do they not see what's inside them projected outward onto others? As Lowell saw his own blood veins crisscrossing the faraway planet of Mars, they see others crisscrossed with their fears of being worthless and inferior."

The Hardest Part

A beginning student asked, "Teacher, I find it so difficult to do my spiritual exercises. Tell me, is the beginning the hardest part?"

"To begin any work," replied the teacher, "may seem to be the hardest part. Yet midway is even more difficult, since we often see few results and can become weary of striving. But the most difficult part in any work comes at the end. It is the last mile of a race that takes the most out of us and really tests our strength."

*In **The Divine Milieu** Teilhard de Chardin writes of finding God in life's diminishments as well as in the abundance of life. Teilhard challenges us to find God in the physical and mental diminishments of our aging, in, "the darkest element and most despairingly useless years of our life." He then expands this quest of finding the sacred in all of life: "Death is the sum and consummation of all our diminishments.... We must overcome death by finding God in it."*

For those who lovingly find God in their physical and mental diminishments of aging, death truly becomes high holy communion.

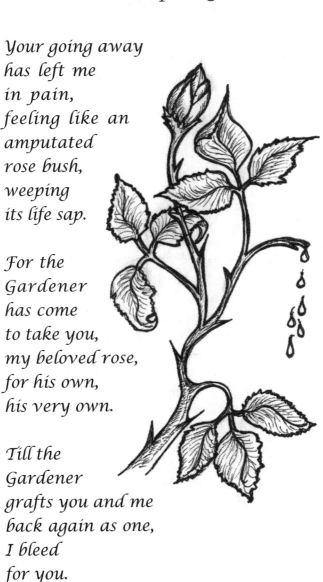

*Your going away
has left me
in pain,
feeling like an
amputated
rose bush,
weeping
its life sap.*

*For the
Gardener
has come
to take you,
my beloved rose,
for his own,
his very own.*

*Till the
Gardener
grafts you and me
back again as one,
I bleed
for you.*

Excommunicated Lovers

A sad-faced, newly married couple came to visit the teacher. "Because I was married before," the husband said, "we had to be married outside the church."

"You mean," the teacher inserted with a chuckle, "you were married on a street corner or in a wheat field?"

"Teacher," the husband replied, "you know what I mean! We were not married by a priest or with the blessing of the church."

"So now we're excommunicated!" his wife added, wiping tears from her eyes. "We can't go to Communion, and we feel so separated from Christ."

"Why?" asked the teacher. "Addressing the Christians in Rome, St. Paul wrote to just such as you when he said, 'And who will separate us from the love of Christ? Shall trial, distress, persecution, hunger, nakedness, danger or even the sword? For I am certain that neither death nor life, angels nor principalities....'" — the teacher paused for a moment and added, "Be aware that even the church might be included among *principalities* — '...will be able to separate us from the love of God that comes to us in Christ Jesus.'"

The husband reached over and took his wife's hand as they looked deeply into each other's eyes. "Now, go in peace," said the teacher blessing them, "and love each other with all your hearts."

Romans 8: 37-39 is truly good news for those who suffer from a sword that tries to separate them from the love of God in Christ. Jesus of Nazareth, who was the living Word of God, was also living Holy Communion for those people in his day whom religion had excommunicated. As God's Uniter, he went about joyfully living out the very words that years later St. Paul was inspired to write.

If you had to choose, which do you think is more pleasing to God: going to Holy Communion or living Holy Communion?

"You will never die," says Jesus, "if death finds you fully alive."

—Fragment 2, Syah Scroll, 5: 8

Burying the Dead

Seeing the teacher walking past carrying an old shovel, the student asked, "Teacher, where are you going?"

"To bury the dead," the teacher answered as he continued walking. "Would you like to come and help me?"

The student eagerly ran after him, "Yes, of course I would, for burying the dead is a corporal work of mercy."

When they arrived at the cemetery, the teacher chose an unused plot and began shoveling feverishly. After having dug down a few feet, he stopped and stepped out of the grave. "Is it my turn to dig?" asked the student.

The teacher eyed the grave and said, "Nope, this grave is finished. It's ready for the deceased."

"But, Teacher," exclaimed the student, "that grave you've dug can't be more than three feet deep — it's far too shallow to bury the dead!"

Wiping the sweat from his brow with a handkerchief, the teacher replied, "Son, those who live shallow lives only deserve to be buried in shallow graves! Only those who have lived deeply are rightfully entitled to be buried six feet, or even deeper, in the earth."

The teacher swung the old shovel onto his shoulder and started walking off. "And the only ones who are truly entitled to be cremated are those who have lived, loved and worked their entire lives as if they were on fire!"

All the way home the student walked behind the teacher in silent reflection as he wrestled with how deeply would they bury him. He began to consider wether he could ever deserve to be cremated.

Addition or Subtraction?

"Teacher," a student proudly proclaimed, "every day I strive to learn something new and to take on some new spiritual task so I can quickly become holy."

"No one," replied the teacher, "becomes holy in a hurry. The best way to become Godlike is not to take on some new work each day but, instead, to drop something daily!"

The ancient scriptures of China say that in the pursuit of learning, "every day something is acquired. In the pursuit of the Way, the Tao, every day something is dropped."[1]

If you had a seven-day drop-off list, what might it contain?

[1] *Tao Te Ching*, Chapter 48

Sick and Tired

"I'm sick and tired of always losing my temper," the seeker said. "Teacher, can you help me learn to be patient."

"Yes," said the teacher who sat in silence for a moment.

"Well," said the slightly irritated seeker, "tell me, then, how do I learn to become patient?"

"Easy," replied the teacher, "you learn by first becoming sick of being sick and tired. Only then will you not be sick and tired."

The holy book of Taoist China says, "The sage is not sick because he is sick of sickness."[1]

Negative behaviors can be changed only when we are so disgusted with them as to take radical action to change them. Attempting to change before we've reached that stage is like a snake trying to shed its skin before the skin's ready to be shed. Yet, when we are truly "sick and tired," we simply slide out of our old skin.

[1] *Tao Te Ching*, Chapter 71

"No one sews a piece of unshrunken cloth
on an old cloak,
for the new will pull away
from the old
and the tear will get worse."[1]

Yet,

soaking

a patch

of God's

new cloth

for centuries

and centuries in

holy water,

will ensure

that the New

can be added

without changing the shape of the Old.

[1] Mark 2: 21

Teach Us to Pray

One day several students came to the teacher, who was praying in a lonely place, and requested, "Teach us how to pray."

"Which would you prefer I teach you," the teacher asked, "an easy prayer or a hard prayer?"

The students had a brief conversation among themselves; then one of them said, "We would like you to teach us a hard prayer."

"Good," said the teacher. "When you pray, do it like this:

> O Beloved, who loves me more
>   than I could ever love myself,
>   help me, for I am a fool and do not know
>   how to ask for what I truly need.
> Beloved, open my heart to you
>   and give me what I need this day:
> Raise me up or strike me down,
>   reward me or punish me.
> Give gifts of shame or fame, disgrace or praise,
>   success or failure, sickness or health.
> I offer myself to you *in* and *as* a sacrifice,
>   so I may joyfully meet
>   all that comes my way this day."

Indeed, this prayer — based on one by the saintly Archbishop Fenelon of Louis XIV's court — is a hard prayer to pray honestly. Yet, praying it at the beginning of a new day would prepare you to respond joyfully to all you might encounter in life as gift, as an answer to a prayer.

The Goat's Hair Monk

The Goat's Hair Monk wasn't a monk, and he didn't wear a goat's hair monk's robe. He was only one of the poor street people who roam the shabby streets of the decaying inner city. He had been nicknamed the Goat's Hair Monk because he went about mumbling to himself, "Goat's hair, goat's hair." The "monk" part came from his routine of going into old St. Martin of Tours Church several times a day to pray. Yet, the old eccentric looked more the part of a friar as he made his daily rounds through the poor part of the city in his drab, ragged clothing.

The old Goat's Hair Monk was not your typical panhandler with his hand always out for charity; instead his hand was out giving away things to the poor. Reaching down deep into the old, battered canvas bag he carried everywhere he went, he would pull out a pair of socks for a streetwalker who had none, a pair of warm gloves for a disoriented bum whose hands were blue from the cold, or a couple of sandwiches for a hungry old bag lady. With each gift, he would beam a big smile and mumble in his heavy German accent, "Goat's hair, goat's hair."

The local street gang members were convinced the Goat's Hair Monk carried a big stash of money in that old bag of his. They had made up wild stories about how he had once been a millionaire who "got religion," went off the deep end and now, carrying everything he owned in a bag, was one of the crazies who wander the city streets.

One day in church the Goat's Hair Monk was sitting with his eyes closed praying in front of a stand of flickering vigil candles beneath a statue depicting holy St. Martin giving half of his cloak to a beggar. Through the dark shadows of the dimly lit church, a kid from the

127

street gang snuck up behind him, confident that the old man had fallen asleep while praying, leaving his bag unguarded in the pew. As the kid reached to snatch up the monk's bag, like a lightning bolt the old man's arm struck with a karate-like blow and his voice thundered out, "God's here!"

The punk kid's face wrinkled prune-like in pain as the old man said, "Wise up, kid! You steal from me or from anyone else, and all you'll get back in life is pain. Rob others and you yourself will be robbed of what's precious to you — that's the ancient law. Now, go, and remember, God's here."

As the kid ran out of the church, he realized the old man hadn't been saying to everyone, "Goat's Hair" but rather "God's here"! About half a block away from the church, the kid looked over his shoulder and saw that members of a rival gang were following him. Attempting to escape, he ran down an alley, only to find it was a dead end. Turning around in fear, he faced several gang members coming toward him armed with baseball bats and knives. Then he remembered and said, "God's here." Two or three drew back as the rest hesitated. So he said it again, louder, "God's here!" Suddenly, the alley was empty.

After that, whenever the kid saw the Goat's Hair Monk going into St. Martin of Tours to pray, he too would go in and kneel beside him. Before long, he asked the old man to teach him how to pray. Soon, he quit the gang and became the old man's bodyguard and disciple, helping him care for the poor. Years later, when the old Goat's Hair Monk lay dying, he gave his old battered bag to the young man, saying, "Remember, son, God's here."

"God's here," would be a good summary of the preaching of Jesus, who by his words and life made the reign of God present in the world. Those two words can also be an awakening prayer before eating a meal, making love, when you are lost or confused, when confronted by evil or danger. What would your life look like if you lived the Gospel of God[1] like the Goat's Hair Monk?

"Sin is a crooked road," says Jesus, "that, by God, leads home, not to hell."
—Fragment 2, Syah Scroll, 5: 22

[1] See Mark 1: 14-15

The Prodigal Son's Brother

The father of the prodigal son died a peaceful death a short time after his wife had drawn her last breath. At his deathbed were both the younger son, who once had been a prodigal, and the elder son, who had obediently served his father all his life.

Upon returning from their father's burial, the elder brother said to the former prodigal, "Give to me the ring that our father gave you at your homecoming, for now it and all his property belongs to me! Years ago on the day you returned home, he assured me that everything he had was mine."

The younger brother slipped off the ring and handed it to his brother. "Now, take off that silken robe and those soft sandals he also gave you — then, get off my property at once. I'm the owner of all of our father's estate — just as he said I would be — and I want you out of here. I hate the very sight of you. You are weak, and you sinfully wasted your inheritance on prostitutes, drinking and gambling. Now, go!"

"But, brother, I have no money," the younger brother pleaded. "On what will I live?"

"You can live," snarled the elder brother, "on your delicious memories of your sin-soaked nights!"

Without a word, the younger brother departed to join the other homeless souls who wandered the roads. That very night the elder brother was awakened from his sleep by sounds outside his open window. Arising from his bed, he went to the window and saw someone digging a hole in his yard. Struck by a paralyzing fright, he recognized the figure as his dead father's ghost!

"Father," the elder brother shouted out the window, "what are you digging?"

"Your grave, my son," the ghost sadly answered.

"Does that mean," the elder son asked, "that I am to die soon?"

"No," moaned the ghost, "you're already dead!"

More deadly than cancer is the virus of revenge.

How to Be Free

"Teacher," said a student, "You frequently speak to us about freedom, so it must be important to you."

"It is indeed," replied the teacher. "It has ever been a key teaching of the great ones. Jesus is the great liberator. Buddha knew how important was freedom, and for Moses the Promised Land was the home of the free and the brave. I believe that Freedom is God's middle name."

"Tell me, then, how do I become free?" asked the student.

"Want nothing," smiled the teacher.

Being grateful at all times and for all things should create an inner world free of the perpetual wanting that makes our society so restless and discontented. Such a powerful, all-encompassing poverty of not wanting is a royal road to freedom.

When the removal of desire is taken to the extreme of not even desiring the next life, it becomes the ultimate revolution. The **Dhammapada** *records the Lord Buddha as saying of the holy person, "He/She wants nothing from this world. And nothing from the next. He/She is free."[1]*

[1] *Dhammapada*, Chapter 26

When the Student Is Ready

Traveling through India, a young seeker complained that he couldn't find a true spiritual master willing to guide him. "When the student is ready," he was told time and again, "the teacher will appear."

On returning to America, he completed college, married, raised a family and built a successful career in business, yet no teacher appeared. Books were his only guidance for prayer, meditation and the spiritual life. Still, whenever famous Eastern gurus or renowned spiritual teachers came to town, he'd always attend their lectures, hoping to find his teacher. Yet, not one of them appealed to him, and the words heard many years before in India continued to haunt him, "When the student is ready, the teacher will appear."

He passed from middle age into retirement years and then into old age, where he finally gave up his quest for a spiritual teacher. When diagnosed with an advanced stage of cancer, he requested to die at home in his own bed. "No need for a teacher now," he said to his favorite grandson, who was youthfully excited about the spiritual quest. As the youth nodded in agreement, a knock came to the door.

"I'll bet that's Old Death making a house call," the old man joked to his grandson. "Go and answer the door, lad."

The young man returned, beaming, "Grandpa, he says he's your teacher!"

When you find yourself

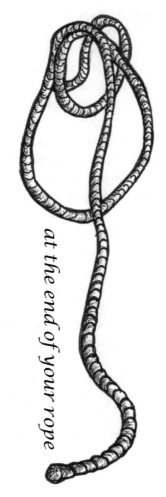

at the end of your rope

you're at a good place to learn how to pray with all your heart.

The Mateless Glove

Shivering in the cold, the old worn-out glove lay in the dirty gutter near a curbside trash can. The cold wind sent scraps of newspaper skipping along the gutter over the discarded, tattered glove. It was easy to see it had been used and abused during its lifetime. Just then, a bum staggering past leaned down and picked it up. But he threw it back in the gutter, grumbling aloud, "What the hell — it's left-handed!"

"I'm worthless, just trash," the mateless old glove mourned. "The only course left for me now is down the sewer or off to the dump. What good am I? I'm of no use for anything." Then the glove did a strange thing: It prayed, "O God, who loves the outcast and the useless, come to the aid of this poor old glove."

Suddenly, the glove sensed itself being lifted up out of the gutter and then felt a warm, strong hand slowly sliding inside it. "What sensual joy, what ecstasy," thought the glove as the hand filled it, "like when a bridegroom enters the emptiness of his beloved."

"Ah, it fits like a glove," said the voice belonging to the hand in the glove. "Now it's time for me to go to work."

Within minutes, the glove found itself cradled under the elbow of a crippled old bag lady who was attempting to cross a busy street. When the glove was raised high with authority, its fingers spread apart, cars, trucks and buses screeched to a stop for the weary woman as she slowly hobbled her way across the intersection.

Then the glove felt itself tapping the shoulder of a well-dressed businessman hurrying down the sidewalk. The executive stopped, looked over his shoulder and then in the direction pointed by the glove: to the door of a homeless shelter that he was passing. The voice of the hand in the glove said, "Why don't you go inside and give them a helping hand?" Surprisingly, that's just what the man did: He went directly inside and presented the homeless shelter a donation of several hundred dollars. "A miracle," thought the glove.

An hour later, the old glove felt itself beginning to turn soft as velvet while the hand inside it grew hard as iron. Then, with a viselike yet gentle grip, the gloved hand squeezed the arm of a young kid about to shoot up with crack cocaine. "Drop it, son! That's poison," spoke the voice of the hand. "Before you kill yourself— change your life. Now!" To the glove's astonishment, the kid threw the crack down the toilet, picked up the phone and called a drug treatment center.

A short while later, the powerful hand in the glove coiled its fingers into a hammer-like claw, which broke apart two men about to begin a fight. With calm and persuasive conviction, the voice of the hand pointed out a way by which both men could walk away from the fight without either losing face. The old glove was overcome with amazement.

"Never," said the glove, speaking to the hand wearing it, "have I felt so happy and so useful as when you've filled me up."

The four fingers of the hand in the glove applauded its palm. "And congratulations on what you've done," replied the hand. "I'm glad you're happy. I certainly am. Because, contrary to what some might think, you and I make a great pair."

Blessed are the humble, those who are truly empty of themselves so that God can fill them to do great things. The humble glove knows that the work it does is made possible by the hand inside it, and so it never boasts about what it does, but only enjoys being filled with the Beloved.

As Paul said, "Consider your own situation. Not many of you are wise, as men account wisdom; not many are influential.... God chose those whom the world considers absurd to shame the wise; he singled out the weak of the world to shame the strong. He chose the world's lowborn and despised, those who count for nothing...so mankind can do no boasting before God."[1]

[1] 1 Corinthians 1: 26-31

Job Qualifications

"Teacher, I'm having a hard time," said a student, "filling out this form for my application to the ministry. Would you please help me?"

"Certainly," replied the teacher, "what's your difficulty?"

"I'm stuck on this question that asks me to list my strengths. I understand how such information is important for determining my qualifications for this work and the gifts I might bring to the ministry. Since you know me so well, how should I answer that question?"

"List your weaknesses!" replied the teacher.

Paradoxically, it is in our weaknesses that we can attain and accomplish the most wondrous marvels, as Paul of Taurus knew: "...for power is made perfect in weakness. I will rather boast most gladly of my weaknesses, in order that the power of Christ may dwell with me."[1] The greatest strengths for the ministry and for any work lie at the core of your weaknesses.

[1] 2 Corinthians 12: 9

The Unworthy Kid Glove

"O Lord, I am not worthy that you should come to me, yet say but the word and I shall be healed," wept the glove whose empty fingers were tightly coiled in a fist. "I am such a wretch, a worthless sinner," wailed the glove as it clutched itself in anguish. "O Lord, I am not worthy that you should come to me, yet say but the word, say but the word."

The unworthy glove was so curled up upon itself that no hand could possibly get inside it. Yet, while no hand occupied the glove, it was not empty! The unworthy glove was filled fat with self-pity. Yet God, who hears the prayers of all who beg, attended to the glove's ceaseless lament, "...say but the word."

"All right, all right," moaned a weary God, "I will say the word — and, kid, the word is *Relax*!"

"Relax?" asked the startled glove as it wiped away a tear. "What do you mean, relax?"

"Relax, let go of yourself. Forget yourself and your precious image of being a wretch, a sinful kid," answered God. "As long as you are stuffed — full of grief over your failings and your unworthiness — there's no room for me, or anyone, to come into you. So, kid, if you want to be healed, relax!"

Front Page Parable

The Dangers of Frequent Bathing

"This is interesting," said the teacher, reading the newspaper. "It's from a news article about researchers at Bristol University in England. They announced the results of a study of 14,000 young people. It concluded that bathing every day is not good for children. According to the study, those who take regular baths are twenty-five percent more likely to develop asthma and other allergies because their immune systems are delicate and still evolving."

"I need a little help," pleaded the student. "I fail to see the parable in that news article."

"I'll give you a hint," said the teacher. "Consider the conventional wisdom of parents and teachers having children frequently go to confession. It may be a pious practice, but is it a healthy one?"

When you cut the chain of religion

keep the anchor

Caution with the Bathwater

One day a student proudly informed his teacher that he no longer was a believer. "Ah, you've seen the light," replied the teacher. "That's wonderful, for those who believe only in themselves are indeed lost."

The student looked shocked. "Teacher, I wasn't talking about believing in myself."

"Excuse me," replied the teacher. "Well, then, I affirm your new disbelief in science. Be an atheist of all that mumbo-jumbo about discoveries — they're just theories anyway. Science keeps changing what it teaches as verifiable truth. One century, it teaches one thing to believe in, and the next century scientists come along with some new discovery and begin to teach the opposite."

The frustrated student interrupted, "Teacher, I'm not talking about science. I am no longer a believer in religion!"

"Oh," answered the teacher with mock wide-eyed astonishment. "Why?"

"What do you mean, why?" replied the student whose face beamed with pride. "I no longer believe in all that nonsense I was taught as a child, that's why!"

"Ah," said the teacher, slowly nodding his head in agreement. "Yes, but be very careful, lest you throw out the baby with the bathwater — especially if you're the baby."

*The holy bathwater of childhood isn't the **real** baptismal bath! As John the Bather said, "I baptize with water, but the one who is to come after me will baptize in fire and the Holy Spirit."[1] Baby's bathwater is far too lukewarm for that fiery plunge of a lifetime. So, for many, the first step toward authentic conversion is to become a nonbeliever in the religion learned as a child. Then the deeper baptism can begin.*

Blest are those who seriously question the religion of their childhood. More blessed still are those who reject it, then set out bravely to seek an adult religious faith. It may have the same name — having its source in the same birthing waters. But it will be a mature and dynamic — if not a dangerous — religious faith.

"Don't be too comfortable," says Jesus, "for then you won't need a liberator."
—Fragment 2, Syah Scroll, 5: 6

---

[1] Luke 3: 16

The Novice's Holy Pain

There was once a young man who found himself possessed by a great burning hunger to be holy. This was no simple craving or passing desire but the aching pain of one who is starving. The youth called his hunger a "vocation."

Eager to do whatever was necessary to satisfy his gnawing hunger and thirst for holiness, he joined a religious community. With clockwork precision the brethren gathered five times daily for communal prayer in the monastery chapel. There they recited psalms, litanies, reflections, meditations, various pious prayers and other devotions. Attendance at these five periods of communal prayer was strictly required for all the brothers. Any other activity during these times was not allowed.

The hungry young man faithfully attended each of these periods of prayer: very early in the morning, mid-morning, noon, late afternoon and the last one at night. Sunday to Sunday, week after week, the prayer times droned on. In time the novice began to experience an unfamiliar affliction. He began to find breathing difficult and struggled with the feeling of being smothered.

These stifling attacks came upon him whenever he was at prayer in the monastery chapel. While the chapel was large and had a high vaulted ceiling with many windows, whenever the novice walked in he'd begin to feel suffocated. One day at the noontime prayer, the novice began violently gasping for breath and then collapsed unconscious onto the marble floor. The prior and four of the brothers quickly carried him outside and laid him on the ground. "Make room, brothers," cried the prior. "Let the lad breathe."

Soon the novice regained consciousness and eagerly inhaled lungsful of fresh air like a rescued drowning man. Slowly sitting up, he protested, "I'm all right. I'm all right. It was just a fleeting spell." The concerned brothers, however, insisted that he go to the monastery infirmary. There he was given instructions to rest.

The novice wasn't tired, and so he sat up in bed and picked up the Bible that was resting on the bedside table. He was causally flipping through Matthew's Gospel, when Jesus' words in chapter 5, verse 6, came flying off the page and seized his heart. He got out of bed at once and that very day left the monastery because now he knew the source of his suffocation.

Walking down the road away from the monastery, the former novice repeated to himself those liberating words of Jesus, "Blessed are those who hunger and thirst for holiness, for they shall have their fill." As he walked along the road, he inhaled deeply the warm, moist spring air, he became aware of an ever-growing thirst.

"The Psalmist says, 'Seven times a day I praise you,'" says Jesus, "but I say to you, praise God seventy times seven times a day."
—Fragment 2, Syah Scroll, 5: 14

Front Page Parable

The Need for Wild Places

"Even the advertisements hold parables for us," said the teacher. "Listen to this Sierra Club ad in the paper with the headline *Wildlife Need Wild Places*. The ad copy reads, 'The alarming decline of America's wildlife and wild lands heritage must be stopped — our future, and that of our children and our planet, depend on it!'"

The student nodded in agreement as the teacher read on, "'We are losing America's plants and animals at an alarming rate due to suburban sprawl, pollution, irresponsible logging and road building — actions which are draining and filling wetlands, leveling our forests, and paving over our prairies.'"

Placing the newspaper on the table, the teacher said, "How true, how sadly true that is for all of us."

Again the student nodded, "Yes, that is a regrettable reality in our industrialized world. But, Teacher, I fail to see it as any kind of parable!"

"A tamed religion is a dead one," said the teacher softly, "and a domesticated God who is no longer wild cannot inspire madness. Yes, the madness of love. Wildlife disciples need wild places to remain wild."

The Leak

"Master, is it necessary to pray frequently?" asked the student.

"Yes," replied the teacher. "For praying is like winding your watch. If you fail to perform that duty daily, your watch will fail you. Allow me to tell a story.

Once upon a time, there was an aspiring young woman whose livelihood involved constantly driving in her car. She was so busy, however, that she never looked at her car's gasoline gauge. This was doubly unfortunate, since her gasoline tank had a slow leak. She drove herself frantically from this to that function, from one task to the next, unaware that she was losing fuel.

In a hurry, she raced past filling stations as she drove herself from task to task. She didn't stop at any of them: One had the wrong kind of gasoline. The next had long lines at the pumps. Another was inconveniently on the wrong side of the road. And she was in a hurry every day.

The highway she was traveling was as flat as a Kansas prairie, and fog shrouded her path as she drove mostly on gas fumes from her now almost-empty tank. Suddenly, however, a high mountain rose upward out of the thick blue-gray fog. As she raced onward up the mountain, still not a third of the way up the steep incline, she coasted slowly to a stop. You guessed it — she was out of gas."

The Garden Mystery

One day, as Adam was whistling while he worked, God was thinking. God thought out loud, "It is not good for man to be alone." At this divine insight, all the animals, birds and fish in Eden nodded their heads in agreement. God smiled.

Adam looked up, also smiling, and asked God, "Why?"

The animals, birds and fish cast sideways glances out of the corners of their eyes toward one another. "Why?" responded God, "What do you mean, why?"

"Lord God," asked Adam, "why is it not good for me to be alone? Being alone, I am able to fully give myself to you and to this work you've given me. So, with all due respect, I suggest that it *is* good for man to be alone!"

The animals, birds and fish all shrugged their shoulders as if to say, "Makes sense. Why shouldn't man live alone?" God did not smile.

"Almighty God," continued Adam, "I love you, for you created me out of a mud ball, filled me with your breath of life and even made me in your image. Alone as your only human creature, I feel so special and so have no need for anyone but you." Adam smiled a self-satisfied grin.

God still did not smile. Time stopped as God thought, but this time not out loud. The animals, birds and fish waited in eager anticipation for God's reply. The garden was silent; the only sound was Adam clipping his fingernails.

Finally, God spoke, "Adam, my delight, you are my unfinished masterpiece. While I wish to complete you, I will do so only if you give your consent. Yes, Adam, you indeed do love me — as far as you can.

However…" God paused, and all the creatures hung in expectation of what was coming next, "…it is not good for you to be alone because you will only truly love me when you can also love someone as I love you!"

Adam shrugged his shoulders. "O.K., God, I consent to being finished. Do whatever you have to. What do I have to lose? But, Lord God, all this talking is making me sleepy. I think I need a nap." And God smiled — a very big smile.

As St. John said, "God is love."[1] So, to be made in God's image is to be made a lover. Adam indeed loved God, yet this was not enough for God. Adam couldn't love like God since, unlike God, he didn't have someone human to love. Adam wasn't fully in God's image, nor was he fully human without loving another.

God gave Adam a partner whom he could love and, in the process, gave him a Godly wound, the mystery of needing to be loved. God longs to be loved. Perhaps the best translation of the original first commandment is God saying, "Love me." God's garden wisdom was brought to fruition by Jesus, who fully united our love of God and our love of others.

[1] 1 John 4: 16

Two-Eyed Meditation

The teacher and the student were walking together one evening as the sun was beginning to set. "Look, Teacher," exclaimed the student, "how beautiful is the sunset. Let us stop and meditate on it in silence. I think that creation is a wondrously glorious prayer, don't you? Isn't this sunset beyond description?"

"I thought you said you wanted to meditate on the sunset in silence?" said the teacher. "Why are you making all these comments?" Then he sat down on the ground and crossed his legs in a yogi lotus position. The embarrassed student silently sat down beside him.

The sun slowly disappeared from view, and the amber sky turned pink and then pale blue as the first stars began to appear. On the southern horizon, the tops of a storm cloud reflected the last colors of the setting sun. The student began to grow restless and peeked at his wristwatch. An hour had passed since the beginning of their meditation. He glanced over at the teacher, who, while his eyes were wide open, was deeply absorbed.

Gradually, the twilight blue sky turned into a blue-black canopy crowded with brilliant stars. Lightning flashed in the south, and sounds of distant thunder could be heard. Still, the teacher and the now very restless student sat in meditation. Finally, unable to remain silent any longer, the student asked, "Teacher, isn't it time for us to return?"

"Ah, how time flies when you're having a good time," said the teacher, slowly standing up. Then he added, "These old legs aren't what they used to be."

The student also stood up slowly as he allowed the blood to return to his legs. "That was a very long meditation. You must have misunderstood, Teacher. I had only proposed that we meditate on the sunset."

"Ah, but that's what we did!" responded the teacher. "You didn't say you only wanted to meditate with one eye."

"Teacher," asked the student, "what is a one-eyed meditation?"

"That's when you simply ponder the golden beauty of the sunset," answered the teacher. "You see the sunset sky only horizontally if you meditate on it with one eye. If you meditate with your other eye as well, however, you're also able to see vertically — and three-dimensionally.

"With two eyes you meditate not only on the sunset but also on the sky. Seeing with two eyes, you can be aware that the sky is constantly changing. A two-eyed meditation on creation enlightens you to the reality that nothing is constant. Everything is forever, even if imperceptibly, changing. Creation is not an art gallery filled with beautiful pictures; it's a motion picture show that's impossible to stop-freeze on any individual frame of beauty."

The two walked on for a while in silence. As a yellow-white moon slowly rose in the eastern sky, the teacher whispered in the student's ear, "Sunset, pale twilight, thunderstorm, star-sprinkled night and now moonrise — many things happening, yet it's always the same sky. Yes, always the same and always changing — just like you and me."

God, the Music Lover

"Teacher," said the disciple, "today, while walking on the road, I passed a Buddhist monk who was singing a hymn. It was most beautiful and inspiring, so I asked him about the words and to whom was he singing. Sadly, Teacher, he said the words of the hymn were those of the Lord Buddha, and it was he whom the monk was praising. I told him he should be praising only the Lord Jesus Christ. I tried to convert him to the truth, but he only went off down the road singing his song."

"You say you found the melody of his song to be beautiful and inspiring?" asked the teacher.

"Yes," replied the student, "but…"

"Good," inserted the teacher, "then, listen only to the melody, not the words. As for whom is being praised — Buddha or Jesus, Shiva or Mohammed — are they not all one in the Great Mystery?"

"All one?" gasped the student.

"Yes, so also are you and that Buddhist monk. 'We being many,' as Paul said to the Corinthians, 'are one body.'[1] Paul could have said: We, being many instruments, are one symphony. Each of us is one of God's unique instruments. So, let not the violins try to convert the trumpets into becoming violins. Rather, follow the baton of the Spirit who is the conductor of the symphony, and play the melody on your instrument with the greatest passion and love."

St. Francis prayed, "Lord, make me an instrument of your peace." Each of us is a musical instrument, and the Spirit of God not only leads us but also blows through us, draws the bow across our strings, pounds on our drum. Be less concerned about the song your instrument is playing and more engaged in playing it with beauty, harmony and passion. Today, make music with the Spirit of Harmony.

"Always do the right thing," says Jesus, "not the correct thing."
—Fragment 2, Syah Scroll, 5: 12

[1] 1 Corinthians 12: 12

The Wedding Vows

The church wedding was beautiful. There were large bouquets of flowers and tall white candles, and a tenor sang "Ave Maria" accompanied by a great pipe organ. The bride was dressed in a long white wedding gown, and her face was hidden behind a veil of Venetian lace.

Meeting with the pastor before the marriage ceremony, the groom and the bride had made two requests: that they could compose their own marriage vows and that the bride could pronounce her vows first. The pastor agreed to both requests.

In the service, when the time of the exchange of vows came, the pastor nodded to the bride, who said,

> I take you to be my beloved. I will love you with all my heart and soul, in sickness and in health, in good times and in bad. I will never forsake you regardless of your infidelity or neglect, and I pledge my love to you forever, for not even death itself can ever separate us.

The pastor beamed; never had he heard such a commitment of unconditional love. Then he nodded to the groom, who said,

> I take you to be my life-partner. I shall not marry another while married to you. I shall never take your name in vain, and I shall visit with you for at least an hour once a week. I shall try not to kill or abuse you or bear false witness by lying to you. I shall not steal from you or covet your possessions, until death do us part.

The pastor then blessed the marriage: "In the name of the Father, and of the Son and of the Holy

Spirit. I now pronounce the two of you to be joined together in the holy covenant of marriage."

Then, to the groom and pastor's surprise, the bride began sobbing.

A good summary of Jesus' teachings can be found in chapters 5, 6 and 7 of Matthew's Gospel. Those chapters contain what have been called the "hard sayings," such as, "Never return injury for injury."[1] These commands have often been judged as impossible requirements for anyone living in the real world. Yet, early Christians thought otherwise, and they struggled to observe these difficult mandates of Jesus.

To ease the difficulty, in the twelfth century a double standard was introduced whereby all baptized Christians were required only to observe the Ten Commandments of Moses. As for the so-called "hard sayings" of Jesus, they were to be observed only by the spiritual elite: monks, nuns, priests and those seeking perfection.

If you really strive to live the commandments found in Matthew's Sermon on the Mount — never becoming angry with another, traveling the extra mile when necessary, never returning injury for injury — you will perpetually fail. If someone asks, "Are you a Christian?" perhaps the correct answer would be, "Not really, but I am becoming one."

[1] Matthew 5: 39

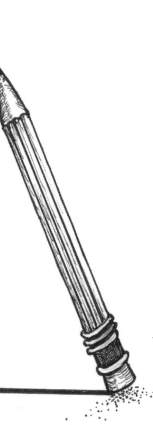

*Blessed
are
the
Graffitists
who
erase—
deface
the
line
between
the
practical
life*

*and
the
spiritual
life.*

Pentecostal Fire

An eager student, tingling with excitement, asked, "Teacher, what do you think about Charismatics? Last night at a Pentecostal prayer meeting I had hands laid on me, and now I'm filled with the fire of the Holy Spirit!"

"As there are many roads to God, so too there are many ways to be gifted by the Holy Spirit," the teacher replied.

The baptized-in-the-Spirit-student then asked, "Teacher, don't you think speaking in tongues and the fiery enthusiasm of Charismatics are wonderful?"

After several moments of silence, the teacher said, "Prairie fires are exciting and colorful, but, alas, they're usually short-lived. The best fires are those in kitchen stoves."

Front Page Parable

Household Ecstasy

The earnest student came to the teacher asking about mystical experiences. "Are they only for the spiritual elite? What must I do so that I can know ecstasy?"

"Your answer is right here on the front page of the newspaper," the teacher said as he folded the newspaper inside out. "It's a news article about Dr. Jean Claude Kaufmann, a sociologist at the Sorbonne University in Paris. He reports that more than half of the one thousand women he surveyed said they found housework pleasurable. Nearly all who worked in their homes said that their housework heightened their emotions in some way, even erotically. One woman in his survey said that she ironed immediately after breakfast to experience 'explosions of joy.' Another became 'inflamed with passion' by touching the 'meanest dishcloth.'

"Now you know," continued the teacher, "why Jesus, like a slave, washed his disciples' feet at the Last Supper and said to them, 'That my joy may be yours and your joy may be complete.'"[1]

[1] John 15: 11

The Taste of Joy

The student said, "Teacher, you are always so joyful; it's a delight to be near you."

The teacher smiled. "Thank you. Are you joyful too?"

Grinning, the student replied, "Yes, I think so."

The teacher replied, "You think so. Why do you *think* you are?"

"I have a nice comfortable home which is air-conditioned," the student replied, "with no mortgage, and it's in a good neighborhood."

"And…?" the teacher asked.

"Let's see, my health is good," the student answered after a moment. "My job is secure with a good company that has a great health care plan."

"And…?" asked the teacher.

"Let's see," said the student. "I also have a nice car, closets full of fashionable clothing, and enough money to take one or two vacation trips a year. So, yes, I think I'm joyful."

"And beyond your good fortune, have you ever *tasted* joy?" asked the teacher, blindsiding the student.

At the Last Supper, the dying wish of Jesus to his disciples was, "that my joy may be yours and your joy may be complete, full to overflowing."[1] Moreover, we are called to a perpetual vocation, "to rejoice always."[2] While good fortune, or any of the circumstances listed above by the student, can cause happiness, are they expressions of joy? What is the source of joy in life, and what creates a lifestyle of rejoicing in all things and at all times?

[1] John 15: 11
[2] 1 Thessalonians 5: 16

The Gold Picture Frame

McBrien's Funeral Parlor was jammed wall-to-wall, and the mourners even flowed out the front door onto the sidewalk. It was the biggest wake anyone had ever seen. Everyone in the long line of mourners waited patiently for his or her turn to pay respects and stand briefly in front of the deceased's simple coffin.

"He looks so natural" was what everyone said looking down at Pat Finnerty. "He looks like he's only sleeping, and not dead," his neighbor commented. "Yes, so lifelike," responded the neighbor's wife, "especially holding his gold picture frame. He was never without it. I'd bet he even took it with him to bed and slept with it." The two bowed their heads in a brief prayer and slowly moved away from the coffin.

Resting in his coffin, old Pat Finnerty wore a smile and his best suit. And, of course, in his hands he held an ornate gold empty picture frame. Like his neighbor's wife, most of those attending his wake could not remember ever having seen Pat without that gold picture frame — eccentric that he was. However, a few of the older folk present could recall the days when Pat didn't carry it with him everywhere he went. They remembered the bad old days, the sad bottle days, of Pat Finnerty the town drunk, a man trying to drown his unhappiness in whiskey.

How Pat escaped from the sea of whiskey and stumbled ashore dry to become the town's gentle eccentric was an unknown story. What everyone did know was that from his first day of sobriety onward Pat carried his empty gold picture frame wherever he went. More importantly, ever since that day no one could recall him being other than happy and cheerful.

Among those whose lives are off-center from the ways of sensible folk, being a happy eccentric is a most rare and welcome phenomenon. The only complaint about Pat was, "It takes Pat Finnerty twice as long as anyone else to do anything." And it did. Even something as simple as going to the grocery store took a long time because Pat was forever stopping to look at things and persons through his empty gold picture frame.

After carefully framing some person, dog or tree, Pat would exclaim, "How beautiful and divinely exquisite!" He used the same phrase whether he was looking at old friends or strangers, at a sleek, expensive Cadillac or a dirty trash truck: "How beautiful and divinely exquisite." While Pat's eccentric behavior caused most of the townsfolk to consider him as one of life's unfortunates, there were folk who secretly envied his perpetual happiness.

A year before Pat's death he was walking past the barbershop. The barber remarked to the man whose hair he was cutting, "Look, Jim, there goes old Pat Finnerty. Lucky man! With his damn empty gold picture frame, he lives every day like he's inside some art museum."

Jim McBrien, the town undertaker, happened to be the man in the barber's chair. He replied, "You're right. Pat's the only man I've ever known in my entire life who's guaranteed to have a happy death."

Fill in the Blank

A disciple asked, "Teacher, when I have to fill out a questionnaire, I don't know what to list as my occupation, since I am primarily a seeker of the truth, regardless of what job I might have at the time. Naturally, I hesitate to list *Seeker* as my occupation. Tell me, what should I write in that blank?"

"In that space provided for your occupation you could write *Preoccupation*," smiled the teacher. "If they ask you what that means, tell them that your daily work is only your hobby and that your main occupation is being preoccupied with Mystery. If they press you, then say you're preoccupied with God."

Each morning as you leave home for your place of employment, make sure that your real occupation is your preoccupation with experiencing God. Be engrossed in God no matter what work you are doing or whom your co-workers are. Being preoccupied is usually viewed as negative, as anti-productive, yet it is the full-time occupation of saints.

Blessed Are the Poor

"Teacher, isn't it absolutely necessary," asked the Bible-clutching student, "to be Christian in order to be saved?"

"Saved from what?" the teacher asked with a smile, "old age, sickness, death?"

"I mean salvation!" snapped the student. "The Bible says that to be saved you must believe in Jesus Christ, for Jesus says…"

"Excuse me," inserted the teacher. "May I ask: Do you believe God desires salvation for all people?"

"Yes, of course," the student replied instantly. "That's why missionary work is so important."

"Christianity has been a great world religion now for two millenniums," said the teacher. "What about those who lived in prior ages? And today only about thirty percent of people in the world are Christians! If God wills the salvation of all, how can Christianity be the only means of salvation?"

"Are you saying Christianity isn't necessary?" the student asked in a hostile tone of voice.

"No, I did not say that," replied the teacher. "Organized religions are, indeed, good; they offer pathways to God. So, follow the path that best fits your feet. As for being saved, did Jesus not suggest the best way to be saved when he said, 'Judge not, and you will not be judged'?"[1]

Gripping his Bible tightly, and without a word, the student stalked out the door. As he was slamming the door, the teacher called after him, "Blessed are those who are poor of religion, for love is theirs."

"Love is theirs": Does this mean that these blest ones are gifted with love or that love is their religion?

[1] Matthew 7: 1

The Dream Team

God was saddened by the many terrible problems facing the planet early in the third millennium after the birth of Jesus. Wars, violence and killing ravaged the world, which also suffered from ecological and psychological violence. Millions faced starvation and killer diseases, while the rich were still exploiting the weak and poor. So global and encompassing were Earth's problems that God realized this time it would require more than a single savior to resolve them. This time the need was so great that God needed a team of saviors.

Earth had many talented God-stars, and each individually was a world-class spiritual champion. Knowing that stars often find it difficult to be good team players, God needed a Dream Team of Spiritual Stars who could work together to save the world. So angelic messengers were sent streaking to the four corners of the world to invite all Earth's God-stars to a Save the World Conference.

In the conference's keynote address, God spoke of the multitude of problems facing Earth, inspiring the corporate passion of the stars, for each had been individually working to solve these problems. God spoke of the New Plan and invited the star-studded collection to become a Dream Team to save, heal and restore the world. After much applause, God left the conference saying, "I leave to you the details of how to implement my New Plan to save the world."

Days grew into weeks, weeks into months and months into years as the God-stars labored over the details of how the Dream Team would implement God's New Plan. Yet, surprisingly, the long delay centered on relatively minor issues. A few of these irresolvable issues were:

1. Deciding on which of God's stars would be the captain of the team.
2. Determining the color of their uniforms and their Dream Team logo.
3. Choosing an acceptable common menu for their training table.
4. Defining the order in which they would sit on the bench.
5. Reaching consensus on which day of the week would be their free or holy day.

As centuries of endless haggling grew into a millennium of meetings, God finally abandoned the idea of a Dream Team of God-stars. Yet because God so loved the world, God did not abandon poor, sick Earth, which now was in an even-worsened plight.

God called a new Save the World Conference and invited a new team to resolve the global problems. It was composed not of spiritual stars but of unbelievers: scientists, scholars, artists and inventors! The angels quickly nicknamed the new team *the UnTeam*.

Is it possible that God would choose nonreligious people to bring the kingdom of heaven to earth? Imagine how the Chosen People of Israel must have felt when Jesus said, "The kingdom of God will be taken from you and given to a people that will produce its fruit"?[1]

[1] Matthew 21: 43

Front Page Parable

English Bus Drivers

"Ah," said the teacher, "here's a news article about a rather common sight along the English countryside. A group of people is waiting at a bus stop as a half-filled bus races past without stopping. All the driver does is wave to them. When the customers later complain to the management of the bus company, they are told, 'Our drivers have strict orders to be efficient and to keep their schedules. If they were to stop for everyone wishing to board their buses, they could never keep their schedules.' End of the news article parable."

"But," asked the puzzled student, "what does it mean?"

"It's a parable that asks a critical question: What is our business? Is it to be efficient or to serve? Now, go for a walk and chew on that good news parable."

The Best Meal Prayer

A certain student invited the teacher to his home to share lunch with him. When the two were seated at the table, the teacher graciously declined the student's invitation to pray and instead insisted that the student say the meal blessing.

It was a long prayer. The student prayed that God would bless those who raised the food, those who prepared it and especially all the hungry who were without food that day.

After the prayer, the student said, "Teacher, I am greatly disturbed that there are millions and millions of hungry in the world today. What are we to do about this terrible problem?"

"Is your next-door neighbor at home?" asked the teacher.

The student replied, "Yes. I believe he is, but..."

"Go and invite him to join us for lunch," said the teacher. "Then ask your neighbor who lives across the street."

"But," the student hesitated, "we only have this small meal!"

"Invite them," said the teacher. "For you will then know the answer to the problem of the world's hungry. That perennial problem was beautifully answered by the Prophet Mohammed, who said, 'Food for two people is enough for three, and food for three is enough for four.'

"Whenever you sit down to a meal, it is good to remember all those who have nothing to eat. However, if you're really concerned about the hungry, sharing your food with them is the best meal prayer."

Going on Retreat

A student carrying a large suitcase stopped at the teacher's door. "Looks like you're going on a trip," said the teacher, eyeing the suitcase.

Pleased at the opportunity to impress the teacher, the student replied, "Oh, no, Teacher, I'm going on retreat."

The teacher asked, "Why?"

"The world is too busy and noisy for me to be in communion with God — and I want to encounter God," the student replied proudly. "So, I'm going off to spend a few days at a lovely mountain monastic retreat center."

The teacher laughed, causing the student to blush pink with embarrassment and say, "I'm sorry, Teacher, I don't see what's funny."

"That suitcase," the teacher said, putting his arm around the student's shoulder. "You're not retreating from the world! You're taking the world along with you into your lovely mountain solitude." Then, pointing his long index finger skyward, he continued, "As the Lord said, 'You can't hide a city on a mountaintop.'[1] If you're really serious about going on retreat, then leave your suitcase — indeed, take off your clothes! Go native, be naked; then you'll make a retreat where you can encounter God."

"Naked!" the student gasped. "The holy monks wouldn't let me in if I appeared naked at their front door! You're not serious, are you?"

The teacher chuckled, "If you want not only the guestmaster but also God to meet you at the front gate, strip yourself of your agenda for your retreat. Unpack your books, tapes and even your Bible. Strip yourself of your habitual ways of how you see, feel and think about yourself, how you think about your daily world and most of all how you think about God. Unpack as well your attachments and preconceptions. Take nothing on retreat except the naked you, the old original you. If you go on retreat in this way — completely naked — be assured that you will encounter God on the mountain."

"The safest time to speak the truth," says Jesus, "is the middle of the night."
                    —Fragment 2, Syah Scroll, 5: 15

[1] Matthew 5: 14

Lord,
let
me
love
you
more
today
than
yesterday,
and
free
me
to
love
you
in
every
way.

The Garden Puzzle

After God had given Eve to Adam as his mate, God told the two that they now needed to become one. Obediently, they did just that. Adam and Eve seemed to be joined at the hip. They were so much in love they couldn't bear being separated. The did everything together — they ate their every meal together, worked together, relaxed together, prayed together and even bathed together. All of Eden rejoiced in their oneness, happy that Adam was no longer lonely.

One day as, hand-in-hand, Adam and Eve were strolling naked together in the Garden of Eden, they heard a voice, "It is not good for one never to be alone."

"What do you mean, dear?" Eve asked, turning to Adam.

"I didn't say anything, my love," a confused Adam replied.

"Well, dear, someone certainly did."

Adam and Eve were no longer naked as they walked back home, for now they were wrapped in a puzzle.

Whether the communal life is one of husband and wife, of monks or nuns or different forms of family, the words of the book of Genesis lead us to the assumption that everything should be done together. Shared meals, work, recreation, conversation are the first word of family and community, but is togetherness the only word?

Healing the Sick

One day the teacher was praying in a lonely place when he heard the noise of a large group of people approaching. He rose from his knees and walked to the edge of the hill to see a great crowd of seekers coming toward him — all of whom had either crutches or canes! Behind them was a band of bodyguards, since the area was known for its dangerous gangs of robbers.

Seeing the teacher standing on the hill, voices from the crowd began crying out loudly, "Teacher, heal us, help us, for we seek to enter the reign of God!"

Upon hearing the idolizing throng, the teacher turned and ran away toward the hills. The mob, on their crutches and canes, come hobbling after him, shouting, "Teacher, we seek to enter the reign of God. Heal us, help us!"

The chase ended when the teacher found himself trapped in a dead-end canyon by the pleading crowd on crutches. "All right, all right," he shouted over their screams, "I'll help you." Then, suddenly, he raced to the rear of the throng and attacked the bodyguards with his stout walking staff, causing all of them to flee for their lives.

"Teacher," the crowd of cripples protested loudly, "what have you done?"

The teacher raised both hands high in the air, signaling for silence. When they were quiet, he said, "Come closer, my children, and I will heal you," and the mass of people eagerly gathered close around him. Quicker than any eye could follow, he raced among them, breaking all the crutches and canes.

Only when no one is guarding your rear and your crutches are broken will you find your way through the eye of the needle of God's reign. Indeed, blessed are those who are vulnerable, for they shall daily dwell in the kingdom of God."

"God is deaf and doesn't read lips," says Jesus, "so speak in sign language."
—Fragment 2, Syah Scroll, 5: 19

The Man in the Bag

One fourth of July the students were arguing among themselves about which of them was the freest. The teacher called them together and said, "Let me tell you a story about the man in the bag:

> There was once a man who awoke to find himself inside prison, yet he had no recollection of ever having committed any crime. Moreover, this was no ordinary prison. No civilized country would ever have tolerated the cruel, inhumane conditions of his imprisonment. The prisoner had been sentenced to a life imprisoned inside a large leather-like bag. Cut into his prison-bag were two small window-holes, through which he could see outside, along with a small slot through which his meals were passed in to him.

> Since it was pitch black inside the bag, it was only by feeling around that he could confirm his suspicion that he was completely alone inside his cell bag. Peering out through the two peepholes, he discovered his bag prison was actually inside an enormous overcrowded prison complex filled with others confined in bags.

> The prisoner attempted to communicate with other bag prisoners the pain of solitary confinement in his bag, but he failed. No one seemed to understand or care — so his painful sense of loneliness deepened. Isolation breeds possessiveness and greed, and so the prisoner in the bag grew more and more selfish, finding it difficult to think of others' needs in the dog-eat-dog world of the prison. Isolation also breeds anger. When other bag-prisoners would hurt him by what they said, he'd attempt to strike back at

174

them, poking at them from within his bag-prison. The prisoner's only consolation was his religion, which gave him a sense of reprieve from his harsh world.

Reading his Bible one day, the prisoner was fascinated by Jesus' words, "the truth will set you free!"[1] Oh, how he longed to be free!

The teacher paused for some time, until one student finally pleaded, "Teacher, please go on! Did the prisoner escape?"

"Well, fellow prisoners," the teacher replied, "he never got out of prison, but he died a free man."

The body is only a prison when we fail to see ourselves as part of the cosmic body of heaven and earth. The prisoner's skin-bag was a prison only because it was isolated, not part of the Body of Christ.

Jesus said, "I have come to set the prisoners free,"[2] and he could have added "from one damn prison after another." Because we are part of the Body, the spiritual life is one of perpetual escapes — from the prisons of isolation into communion, selfishness into generosity, anger into love. Though imprisoned by social or financial limitations, by serious illness or old age, we are ever called to be free — until finally we escape from the last and greatest prison: death.

[1] John 8: 32
[2] See Luke 4: 18

The Chain Gang

Prisoners Working in This Area read the large orange sign strangely posted at a busy downtown intersection. Strange, since such signs — while not unusual in rural areas where prison chain gangs are used to clear brush — seem out of place in a business district.

Chained work gangs were once deemed cruel. Yet, as with capital punishment, chaining prisoners to one another and forcing dehumanizing labor on work gangs is commonly considered morally appropriate. This change of conscience might suggest an attitude that convicted criminals shouldn't get off easily in paying for their offenses. As the old folk adage says, "What's good for the goose is good for the gander."

Prisoners Working in This Area read the sign at the bottom of the chilly, gray canyons of tall office buildings, but none of the prisoners on the sidewalks saw the sign. Indeed, the sidewalks were filled with chain gangs of men and women prisoners hurriedly herded to and from their work areas. As they pressed forward, most had long ago ceased dreaming of parole. They also knew that only one in a thousand ever escaped. Among the shackled, some had convinced themselves they actually enjoyed being prisoners. The rest gritted their teeth, iced their eyes and accepted their fate with only a faint hope of retirement.

Retirement was like a pardon from the governor, a ticket to that faraway Promised Land of freedom. Those lucky enough to live long enough to cross over the Jordan of the Job-World into the land of milk and honey, however, usually still wore their chains. Like jewelry, if you wear work chains long enough you forget you have them on.

So, regarding society's return to chain gangs: What's good for the goose is good for the gander.

176

Front Page Parable

Blind But Not Deaf

"Here's an interesting parable," commented the teacher. "It's in a newspaper article that quotes from *Worth* magazine. It says here, 'In California's Huntington Beach jail, lawbreakers with money can upgrade their accommodations. If you'd like a larger, private cell and better food, all it will cost you is $100 for the first night and $65 a night thereafter.'"

"A parable?" the perplexed student asked. "About what?"

"Criminal justice." replied the teacher. "Indeed, the statue of Lady Justice shows her as blindfolded, but she's obviously not deaf!"

"Not deaf?" asked the student. "To what?"

"The tinkle, tinkle of hard cash," answered the teacher. "Capital punishment is only for those without capital, without money. The rich can hire the best lawyers in the land. I ask you: How many millionaires are to be found in prison, and how many are ever executed for deadly crimes?"

Following Jesus

A seeker came to the teacher with this request: "I want to be holy. I know that Jesus is the doorway to God. Tell me the way to follow Jesus!"

The teacher raised an eyebrow, "Which Jesus? You have a choice: You can follow the Jesus of the theologians, or you can follow the Jesus of the Gospels. The first way is as safe as going to church — and the second way is as dangerous as hell."

The Statue

The student asked, "Teacher, if you could have only one statue in your church, which would you choose: a statue of Jesus, of the Mother of God or of a saint — and which saint?

The teacher smiled, "In my church I would want the Statue of Liberty."

The Way of Freedom
is a spiral path

that gets
narrower
and
narrower
and
narrower

till
there
are
no
more
choices.

The Devil's Workshop

The student stopped at the teacher's open doorway, saying, "Excuse me. I'm sorry to bother you, but I need…"

Seated in a chair, looking out the window, the teacher turned and said, "Come in, come in. You're not bothering me, I wasn't doing anything."

The student joked, "You'd better be careful, Teacher. For remember that idleness is the devil's workshop."

Smiling, the teacher only raised his long index finger — the signal that a story was brewing.

One day, a preacher came upon a peasant wearing a large sombrero and sitting under a tree doing nothing. The preacher shook his finger at the peasant and said, "Wake up, my good man! It's later than you think. Get on your feet and go to work. Don't you know that idleness is the devil's workshop?"

The man raised the brim of his sombrero with his index finger and peered up at the preacher, "Go away! Can't you see that I am busy?"

"Busy!" snapped the preacher. "I'm no fool! Who are you trying to kid, you lazy bum? Sloth is a sin that cries out to heaven for vengeance. So get up and go to work and do something productive!"

Tipping down the brim of his sombrero, the man replied, "I am working. God and I are busy working together on a secret project."

"Blasphemer!" screamed the preacher as he raised his big black Bible high overhead. "Lord God, I pray that you forgive this wretched sinner after you scourge him with the whip of your grace so that he'll come to his senses and change his sinful, slothful ways."

"Go away!" the reclining man replied, this time without raising his sombrero. "Go find someone who isn't busy to preach to. Stop pestering me while I'm busy in God's workshop doing nothing."

It is truly a paradox that it requires far less effort to do something than to do nothing. Especially for those of the Western world, to sit and do nothing requires enormous effort and discipline. If you think it's easy to do nothing with God, then try working at it in God's Sabbath workshop for only ten minutes!

The Camel

"Teacher," said the student. "May I ask: Who was your teacher?"

You may find this difficult to believe," the teacher replied, "but my spiritual master was a camel."

"Did you say, 'a camel'?" the stunned student asked. "Or did you perhaps say 'a Carmelite'?"

"No, not a two-legged monk of the Holy Order of Mount Carmel," the teacher replied. "My master was indeed a four-legged camel, like those you see in an Arabian desert, at the zoo or in a circus."

Curious, the student inquired, "Please, Teacher, explain to me how a camel could have been your spiritual teacher."

"One day, I went to the circus," the teacher said, "and had a good seat right at ringside. The circus band played the Grand Entrance March as all the elephants, tigers, lions, dancing horses, acrobats, tumblers, clowns and camels paraded around the ring. There were seven camels with riders costumed as Oriental kings. When the last camel passed by my seat, it turned its head and looked me straight in the eye with the kind of look that strips you naked.

"I leaped over the low railing and ran after that camel. I was just a few feet from it when two clowns grabbed me and escorted me to the exit, saying, 'Sorry, Mister. Customers aren't allowed in the ring. Insurance regulations. Have a nice day!'"

"But, Teacher," the student interrupted, "how can a simple look, especially a mere glance from a camel, give enlightenment?"

"Who's enlightened?" laughed the teacher. "The best any of us can hope for in this life is to be lightened up. The Way, for me, is like being one of those three-way light bulbs that click-click-click grows brighter with each turn of the switch. Now, in our case it's click-click-click-click-click…."

"But your camel, Teacher! Didn't you go in search of it?"

"I did, you're right. Now, where were we? Oh, yes, outside the tent. So, naturally, I went searching for the camel. I found the seven of them waiting to be fed. It wasn't difficult to recognize the camel who had looked inside me. And the camel recognized me too because it lowered its head down to the level of mine. So I said, 'Tell me your secret.' The camel leaned closer and whispered in my ear, 'I've passed through the needle's eye.'

"Naturally, my first thought was: It's impossible for such a large animal to squeeze through something as tiny as the eye of a needle. Yet, I knew with God all things are possible, so I asked, 'Can you tell me how you accomplished that?'

"The camel again whispered, 'I shrank myself as skinny as a sewing thread.'"

While the term "threadbare" usually refers to frayed and shabby clothing, it could be a new adjective to describe a saint, one who has learned to be skinny as a thread. Those whom fate or fortune has chosen to reside in the first world live in great affluence. As the wealthy of the world, it would be a blessing for them to learn the art of being so threadbare-skinny as to be able to slip through the eye of a needle.[1]

[1] See Matthew 19: 24

The Car

One day the teacher was approached by a young student. "Teacher, I feel that God is calling me. I think I have a vocation to serve God."

"You are fortunate to feel you are called, to feel you have a vocation," replied the teacher.

"Yes, I thought so too," the student answered proudly, "since many are called, but few are chosen."

"Everyone who is born is called," replied the teacher, "and in a sense everyone is at the same time chosen — given not only a lifework and purpose, but a destiny. Yet, of those chosen, few choose to choose."

The student wore a puzzled look and asked, "Teacher, you confuse me — what does that mean?"

The teacher smiled and began a story:

Once a father gave his son a brand new car. It was sleek and beautiful. It had leather seats, a marvelous stereo system and was filled with the latest computer technology. Moreover, the car was complete with a huge 408 V-8 engine capable of great speeds. The son was so proud of his car. Each day as he drove to and from school he felt he was the most fortunate person in the world.

After he finished school, he took his prized car out a couple of times on the freeway and drove it at speeds thirty miles an hour over the speed limit. While this was exhilarating, the car was actually capable of much higher speeds. However, the enormous potential power of the vehicle frightened the young man.

As the years passed, he thought his car was so beautiful and comfortable that he began to live in it. It was not a conscious choice but rather a decision that occurred gradually. He began to drive it less and less, and more and more he ate and slept in his car. In time, the car's tires lost air and went flat, which by then didn't really bother him since he never drove the car anymore. The once-sleek racing engine grew rusty, and families of mice built their nests in it. The battery went dead, the oil seals dried out and the engine hoses cracked.

However, the car's plush leather interior remained as comfortable as ever. The young man, now middle-aged, no longer desired to go racing wildly with the wind. Indeed, all he wanted was to enjoy his comfortable car, to sink deeply into its soft leather seats, close his eyes and listen to the stunning stereo system. As a matter of fact, what he most enjoyed about his car was that it wasn't going anywhere!

Is your vocation or spiritual path going anywhere, or has it become a comfortable, safe dwelling place?

Front Page Parable

Cafe Ke'ilu

"Here's a parable from the International Section of the news," said the teacher as he read. "Cafe Ke'ilu recently opened in a trendy section of Tel Aviv, in Israel. This cafe has tables with linen tablecloths, chairs, plates, silverware, waiters and menus, but it serves no food or drink. The manager, Nir Caspi, explained that people come to his cafe not to eat any actual food, but rather only to be seen and to meet people. The menu is marvelous, having been designed by four-star chef, Phillipe Kaufman. Cafe Ke'ilu's menu allows diners to order some of the world's most exquisite dishes, which would be served to them on elegant, but empty, plates."

The student sat in confusion, so the teacher asked, "Does that remind you of any churches you've visited recently?"

It's a waste of time standing on the dock, waiting for your ship to come in —

unless

you've sent one out.

The Holy Itch

"Teacher," pleaded the student, "Help me satisfy the great hunger I feel for God."

"Is what you feel truly a hunger," asked the teacher, "or only a spiritual itch?"

"I'm confused, Teacher," replied the student. "You say a spiritual itch? What did you mean?"

"Be careful how you proceed," said the teacher. "A hunger is a deep longing that is not easy to satisfy. An itch, on the other hand, is irritating and wants to be scratched, but doesn't last for long. Moreover, there are many who are eager to make money by selling you their special brand of Itching Oil. And if your irritation can be met by their wares, you aren't dealing with a real hunger."

Jesus called blessed those who are hungry for holiness.[1] Indeed, blessed are they, for their hunger shall grow more intense the more they try to feed it.

"Give us this day our daily bread," says Jesus, "and lead us not to nibble on fortune cookies."
—Fragment 2, Syah Scroll, 5: 5

[1] See Matthew 5: 6

The Pot on the Stove

"Teacher," the student said, "I read in a spiritual book that only by becoming nothing can one return to God. So, I seek passionately to become nothing."

"That's indeed a rare desire," replied the teacher, "for in this world everyone wants to become a somebody. So, you seek to become a nobody?"

"Oh yes," replied the student, "A real nobody."

"Ah," beamed the teacher, "you seek the ancient secret of becoming a real somebody where nobody is at home! More often, seekers pretend to be nobody so they can become a somebody. So, be cautious and be sure to start at the beginning. For unless you first become a somebody, it is most difficult to become a real nobody."

"I'm sorry, Teacher," replied the student, "but you've lost me. In a simple way please tell me how to become nothing — which I hope is that 'ancient secret' of which you spoke."

The teacher closed his eyes, pondering as he hummed a Broadway show tune. Then, opening his eyes, he looked deeply into the student's brown eyes, saying, "A simple way. All right, become like that old pot filled with water on the stove. If you turn up the flames as high as possible, I assure you, you will evaporate!"

"Teacher," the student asked as his eyes filled with dread, "doesn't that take time, and isn't such an intense fire painful to the pot?"

"Certainly it does, and certainly it is," answered the teacher.

Teacher to Teacher

"Teacher, your apples have worms!" said the visiting teacher. "I fear you teach what is not orthodox, not solidly from our tradition. Your stories are filled with novelties to tickle the ears and trick the hearts of the simple faithful."

"Thank you, brother," the teacher replied, "for your fraternal correction and your guardianship of orthodoxy. It is clear that you have great concern for the fragile faith of the faithful."

"That was a most gracious response, Teacher," answered the visiting teacher. "I must say, you always live your teaching. Will you not, then, remove from your apples the ugly worms of heresy?"

"Dear brother," the teacher said, "I am sorry, but I cannot. You see, I am a firm believer in a balanced diet. So, along with the fruit of my apple stories comes a little red meat."

As the disturbed visiting teacher left, shaking his head, the teacher said, "As it is said, 'An apple with a worm a day keeps the devil away.'"

Front Page Parable

Nail 'em, and Teach a Lesson

"Ah, yes, 'the oppressed indeed do learn from their oppressors,' to quote a Liberation theologian," said the teacher. "Listen to this report from Russia, which is taken from the January, 1999 *London Tablet*. It states that the Russian State Commission appointed in 1995 by President Boris Yeltsin has released its report on religious oppression in the early days of Communism. The report says that 200,000 Russian Orthodox priests, monks and nuns were killed in Communist purges prior to World War II. In the years following the 1917 revolution, while most were shot or hanged, many died when Communist antireligious death squads crucified them on the doors of their churches.

"The report quotes a top-secret message by Lenin to the Soviet Politburo urging officials to kill as many 'reactionary clergy representatives' as possible. This was to be done with 'frenzied and ruthless energy' in order to teach the people 'such a lesson that they will not dare think about any resistance.'"

The teacher laid down the newspaper and sadly said, "How many brilliant theologians or zealous prophetic pastors in every age have been nailed to their church doors as a lesson to others not to stray from the party line. Yet the docile faithful sheep go in and out of those church doors to pray and worship, blind to those who had been nailed on them."

What Will God Say?

The teacher and two students were reflecting on Jesus' parable of the Last Judgment, in which the king says to the sheep — those who did good in life — "Come, enter into your eternal reward," and to the goats — those who failed in life — "Depart into eternal punishment."[1]

"At the final judgment," the teacher asked, "what do you want to hear God say to you?"

The first student answered, "I would like to hear God say, 'I forgive you. All your sins have been wiped completely away.'"

The second said, "I would like God to say to me, 'Don't worry about all you failed to accomplish in life. I understand. Now, enter into your eternal reward.'"

After a moment, the first student asked, "And, Teacher, at the end of your life, what do you want to hear God say to you?"

The teacher paused, then smiled and said, "I would like to hear God say, 'Thank you!'"

In God's grace, each person has a unique destiny that, when lived out fully, brings the divine dream closer to becoming a living reality. No single destiny is insignificant to that dream, and so the Divine Dreamer longs to see each human life lived to the fullest.

[1] Matthew 25: 34, 41

What If?

The teacher's students came as a group to express their concerns about him. "Teacher," began one of them, "as seekers of God, your teachings bring us joy; they are welcome, fresh good news in our lives. But we are concerned, for there are some who find your teachings to be unorthodox — even bordering on heresy! Surely, they write letters to the authorities complaining about you. We are worried about what the church might do to you!"

"My teachings," the teacher replied, "are not heresy, and they are not orthodox. They're heterodox, which means, 'another orthodoxy.' As you know, I believe that truth comes in more ways than one!"

"But, Teacher," another student spoke up, "what if the church does as it has done so often before and silences you?"

"Silences me? What do you mean?" the teacher asked, smiling. "I thought this was a free country? In 'the glorious freedom of the children of God,'[1] does not each of us have the sacred right of free speech?"

"That may be," a student answered, "but they can still forbid you from speaking and preaching in church."

The teacher only chuckled and responded, "Who listens to anyone speaking in church?"

"But, Teacher, what would you do," the concerned student continued, "if the church were to punish you personally?"

The teacher smiled and responded, "What would I do? I would throw a party and begin to dance an Irish jig." His reply about throwing a party shocked his students, so he went on, "Yes, a party for all of you and other friends so we could rejoice. I believe

Jesus left till last the best of all his beatitudes when he said, 'Blessed are you when they insult you and persecute you, and utter every kind of evil against you because of me. Rejoice and be glad, for your reward in heaven will be great.'"[2] Then, the teacher started humming as he began dancing a colorful Irish jig.

"Teacher, don't joke!" another student said. "This isn't funny! We love you, and we're concerned that sooner or later they will ban your books, ordering that they be destroyed. They might even excommunicate you. What would you do then?"

He stood up, bowed to his students and said, "Well, that's easy. I would communicate them!"

[1] Romans 8: 21
[2] Matthew 5: 11-12

*To your deep inspiration which commands me to be, I shall respond by taking great care never to stifle nor distort nor waste my power to love and to do. Next, to your all-embracing providence which shows me at each moment, by the day's events, **the next step to take and the next rung to climb**, I shall respond by care never to miss an opportunity of rising toward the level of spirit* (author's emphasis).

—Teilhard de Chardin,
The Divine Milieu

Those who only

<u>hear</u> the Word

NVLLAM CAVSAM
MORTIS INVENIO
EO CORIPIAM ERGO
ILLVM ET DIMITTAM·D

need never fear
being charged with
subversive Messianism.

In memory of
Anthony de Mello, S.J.,
Jesuit priest of India,
author, storyteller and spiritual guide
who died in 1987.

May he rest in peace,
unmolested by grave robbers
and vandals defacing his memory,
and may he shine brightly
in the galaxy of the saints of heaven
for his inspiration to many
on earth.

Index Guide to Parable Themes

Rungs on the Ladder
Acknowledgments

Just as a ladder in constructed of many rungs or steps, so is the story of creating this book entitled *The Ladder*. The first step was invisible at the time. I was having lunch in Lawrence, Kansas, with **Trey Parker**, an artist friend from New York City, who had just returned to Kansas to visit friends. Over a beer, Trey spoke of how he had begun telling his friends in New York some of the parable stories from my books.

I was surprised and pleased at how he had used my stories. And I found myself sharing with him an unspoken desire to create short, insightful parables as had the late **Anthony de Mello**. I had always admired de Mello's great artistry of being able, in a few crisp lines, to create wonderful parables that easily lent themselves to retelling.

I came to the second rung of the creative ladder several days later around 3:30 in the morning. I was awakened by the thunder and lightning of a brain-storm. A flood of ideas for short parables flowed from the womb of the Holy Storytelling Spirit. Delighted, I danced out of bed and began to write.

I express my gratitude to an old friend, **Father Walter Heeney, OSB**, a monk of Conception Abbey, whose original inspiration for the character of Abba Syah provided the third rung of the ladder.

The next step came a month later with the help of another gift of the Inventive Holy Spirit — a laptop computer I had taken along on vacation. The vacation's creative empty space allowed the parables to write themselves. After my return, this process continued off and on, sandwiched between other obligations, over the next several months.

The next critical step was handing over my manuscript to my good friend and editor, **Thomas Skorupa**. This ladder rung can be a most difficult one for authors who find it painful being subjected to an editor's scalpel. Yet as Arthur Plotnik said, "The editor's art is to let the fire show through the smoke." Through Tom's smoke-clearing craftsmanship, the parable-stories of *The Ladder* began to be ablaze.

The next step in *The Ladder*'s construction came when my good friend and publisher, **Thomas Turkle**, from his years of experience and great love of books, made decisions that enhanced the quality of this book. Then, closely on the heels of this rung, came the next step, the printing and binding of the book by **Steve Hall** and the talented people of his company.

The final step was your bookseller graciously providing you with an opportunity to acquire this book of parables — a creative process that had begun quite innocently and unconsciously one summer day over lunch with a friend. I express my deep gratitude to each and every person who helped build *The Ladder*.

Edward Seanachee Hays

The author says he was a gifted child, having been born in 1931 B.T., Before the advent of Television! While the radio was not yet ten years old, it could boast of new built-in antennas and speakers instead of the old large speaker horns. Since it was pictureless, the author credits the radio with having sparked his imagination. Radio mysteriously made music or a storyteller present in every living room, and the author believes it was radio that awakened the *seanachee* (shawn-a-key) that lay slumbering in his Irish DNA code.

A *seanachee* is a storyteller. Once, every Irish village had such a person whose enchanting voice could weave the magic of stories. Spiced with mirth, within each story's shell was hidden a nut of wisdom. Even the Irish king had his *seanachee* who was court poet and bard, singer of great heroic legends and teller of spellbinding tales.

His family dinner table and especially the front porch on warm summer nights became the author's classrooms for the art of storytelling. It was on these stages that his parents, uncles and aunts spun tales out of the tapestry of their daily lives during the 1930s Great Depression. Their colorful stories about their relatives, both living and dead, created for the author the fabric of family legends and history.

As an adult he is ever grateful that these childhood influences were graced to be ordained by the Sacred Story Spirit — in awe that the ancient priesthood of storyteller was present in his young life. That same Spirit of God inspired Jesus of Nazareth in his perennial parable stories and was the Holy Ghostwriter of the world's greatest storybook, the Bible.

But you say you don't want a story — just the facts? The facts: After his foundational learning at home, Edward Hays' primary and secondary education was in public schools and his seminary and theology education was at Conception Seminary, Conception, Missouri. He spent his first thirteen years as a Catholic priest in parish ministry, the next twenty-five praying — two of them as a traveling pilgrim and twenty-three as director of a house of prayer. His last three years have been spent in prison. Yes, prison! He presently is the priest chaplain at the Kansas State Penitentiary in Lansing, Kansas. As the new millennium begins, the old storyteller is standing on the windswept ridge of retirement, after which he will…. Ah, but that's a story for another time.

Front Page Parable

Where Do You Live?

"Ah, listen to this," the teacher said from behind his folded newspaper, "it's an article about Frank Sinatra. He's quoted here talking about a woman singer whom he admired and whose style he incorporated into his own. Sinatra said, 'She lived inside the song. It didn't matter who wrote the words or the music.' The writer of the article goes on to say, 'and Sinatra did the same. He inhabited a song the way a great actor inhabits a role.'"

The teacher laid aside the newspaper, saying, "Remember that, for it's a great lesson in a few words about how you can become a good storyteller — or a good teacher, minister, parent, prophet, spouse…! Like Sinatra and his songs, inhabit the story you're telling or the Scripture passage you're reading; live in it regardless of who wrote it.

"So, before you begin to tell any story, always check to see where you're living at that moment."

Sharing These Stories with Others
How to Be a Storyteller

The stories and parables in this book are for personal reading and reflection, but they are also intended for telling. Most people mistakenly believe that storytelling is an art that requires a special talent. This is not true.

I've never met anyone yet who isn't a good storyteller, as long as the story is a personal story. The more sensational the event that happens to someone — a car accident or fire — the more colorful a storyteller that person becomes.

If you desire to tell the stories in this book, don't memorize them! Live them out as if they actually happened to you. In your imagination recreate the words and actions of each character in the parable-story.

Don't be concerned about the small details. If, as an actor or actress, you play the part of each character of the story with as much enthusiasm as you can, I promise you the story will come alive. As you tell it, forget those who are listening, forget yourself and become the story. Simply remember the key events and know well the opening and closing of the story; then let your creativity connect the beginning and the end.

Storytelling is perhaps our most ancient form of communication and education. Storytelling is in your genes, scribbled in your DNA. All you have to do is reawaken that natural gift.